Barack Obama: Ready, Fit to Lead

Road to the White House

BY

Frederick Monderson

authorHOUSE®

AuthorHouse™
1663 Liberty Drive, Suite 200
Bloomington, IN 47403
www.authorhouse.com
Phone: 1-800-839-8640

First published by AuthorHouse   12/22/2008

ISBN: 978-1-4389-4125-7 (sc)

Printed in the United States of America
Bloomington, Indiana

This book is printed on acid-free paper.

Cover Photo. Senator Barack Obama addresses the Congressional Black Caucus. Photo by B. Twilly.

TABLE OF CONTENTS

Senator Obama Addresses the Black Caucus
Foundation, Inc. Photo by B. Twilly.

BARACK OBAMA: AN INTRODUCTION

BY DR. FRED MONDERSON

When Barack Obama burst on the scene about two years ago, many people were unaware of who he was and wondered if he had the wherewithal to, not simply contest the Democratic Presidential Primary and the Presidential Campaign, but to win at least the first, much more both. Well, he persevered and won both by deploying an unbelievable campaign strategy and organization that, working in tandem with the internet allowed him to raise hundreds of millions of dollars, coordinate a successful national campaign strategy and amass a seven million member volunteer database of individuals, who would respond at short notice to act on the candidate's behalf.

It is interesting how Senator Barack Obama astonished the media and pundits as he maneuvered along the arduous trail of the American Presidential campaign turf. One particular act of Barack Obama that amazed many people, particularly the pundits, and generated much discussion, was his announcement of the choice for Vice President. His campaign office stated "The Senator will announce his choice for Vice President via text messaging," which he did some time after that midnight. Many criticized this strategy, rather than, say, like making an announcement at a press conference on the Courthouse steps. Later, when Pres-Elect Obama revealed the size of his database, then everyone began acknowledging the brilliance of the man and his campaign strategy in this and so many other ways. As more and more time passed, people seemed to line up to praise the first African American candidate now about to ascend the stairs in a journey to the White House.

Down to the wire, when everyone vied for the independent vote, and the undecided seemed to hold the election in balance, the incredible candidate kept extolling his supporters to remain vigilant, pay little attention to the polls, do not let up, and vote early, help others vote, knock on doors, make phone calls, and work unrelentingly until the polls close. That insistence paid off handsomely.

Still, there was a nervousness in the air and as the pundits debated the pros and cons of the phenomenal "Bradley Effect," one could imagine the campaign reaching into its bag of confidence saying to its people stay on directive, stay on message, as they ran out the clock. Dr. Ron Walters, the Distinguished Leadership Scholar, writing in the *Daily Challenge*, "My Take on the Bradley Effect," Wednesday, October 15, 2008, p. 4, wrote: "I have been in the camp which says that the Bradley Effect may determine the election, to the point that I doubted Michele Obama who told Larry King on his TV show recently that if there was a Bradley Effect, Barack Obama would not have won the primary election. Trying to reconcile various strains of this complex issue, the primary elections do not stand as something of a refutation that is a Bradley Effect in play, but looking deeper, there are other things as well." Then he mentions two categories of voters, the "emotional" and the "fed-up." Arguing that the Bradley Effect will be muted, Ron Walters cites several factors to justify this view. These were (1) the emotional context that undercounts black voters; (2) the Democratic registration advantage showing more Democrats, young and old, were registered than Republicans; (3) young voters will be instrumental; and (4) a decrease in Black Republicans voting for that ticket. This led Dr. Walters to conclude: "Race is present in this election to the point that every survey this year has told us that whites and Blacks still see things very differently in society and that where this election is concerned, there is a strong segment of voters who will use race to vote negatively."

Even further, he noted: "So, I am not deluded, the Bradley Effect will be at play, but this is a very special election that is moving many people to consider things more important to them than race. This means than in an election that was more "normal" the Bradley Effect could be determinative, but my take is – not this time."

Through it all, Obama assembled a fantastic foreign policy team as well as a domestic policy team. He tapped into the reservoir of "wise men" from the Clinton era; and he surrounded himself with some of the best and brightest scientific, technological, business, and economic minds in the country, as well as top military brass. He listened to them, heeded their advice, learned from them and then demonstrated his increasing knowledge whether in debates, news conferences or on the campaign stump. This is why some pundits called him a transformational figure; a sage, wise person who knows how to listen; who will initiate new ways of thinking about the United States Government and its relationship within country and with the world. Even more, Obama worked unrelentingly to bridge racial, generational, technological, regional and party divides. He extolled his reaching across the aisle in the Senate in a spirit of bipartisanship, consensus building, campaigned in most states and became a winner in both red and blue states. Then he reminded people of the sacrifices of his grandmother, and how she taught him the fundamentals of good citizenship and encouraged his educational development. These traits helped enhance his social, intellectual and political development. One has to believe in his mind, he never forgot the Civil Rights Movement, before, during and after its experiences.

However, and never forgetting his big boost by Senator Edward Kennedy, Obama brought out his big guns, Bill and Hillary Clinton and Al and Tipper Gore, as well as Senators Kerry and Schumer and Governors Patrick, Rendell, etc., and Hollywood actors Will Smith, Matt Damon, and rappers in the Hip-Hop generation, who all campaigned across the country and in the critical battleground states and this helped tremendously. So much was riding on the shoulders of Senator Obama, so many were looking to their leader for inspiration and throughout it all, his cool demeanor handled it well.

Personally I think the Florida victory can be credited to the Clintons. Sure Senator Clinton campaigned there but the former President's appearance carried as much weight. This was particularly evident as Bill Clinton voiced his support for Obama in a late night rally in Kissimmee,

Florida, where the former President praised the future President by telling the crowd, "Barack Obama represents America's future and he will take America forward." Then he told the crowd to "vote and make your friends vote; and, find people still undecided and convince them to vote for Barack Obama." Bill Clinton further explained to the gathering, four reasons why they should vote for Barack Obama. These are philosophy, policy, decision and the ability to execute decisions to make changes in people's lives. These qualities Obama possessed, Clinton told the crowd. "Most important, his philosophy was right for America. He has the right policy that really matters what people think. On Barack Obama's To-Do-List, he has a better economic plan and a better educational plan. He has a better energy plan and is a better decision maker. He is a decider-in-chief who wants to understand, can understand, and this makes him the right choice for America." Former Vice President Al Gore made the voters realize how each vote was really important, and exhorted them to vote for Barack Obama.

When all was said and done, Barack Obama won the election by the largest majority since Lyndon B. Johnson in 1964. He not only won in both red and blue states, on both coasts, but also in the middle of the country. Significantly, he reached out to a broad coalition of diverse groups. This is evident since Obama received 96% of African American votes; 67% of Latino votes; 66% of youth votes; and 66% of new voters.

While its generally agreed Obama has to deliver on the "details," let's not forget he campaigned on a platform where he wanted to:

- Roll back the Bush Administration tax cuts for the wealthiest Americans of whom President Bush had called his "base."

- Give the middle class tax cuts to alleviate the current situation.

- Extend unemployment benefits, increase in food stamps and initiate construction jobs to stimulate the housing industry.

- Start hiring for infrastructure repairs of bridges, roads, tunnels, harbors.

- Build many new schools, upgrade older ones, and provide them with science, arts and technology equipment, and pay teachers more while demanding greater accountability from them also.

- Naturally, the disabled will get their ample consideration.

With this platform of issues, unrelenting campaigning and exhortation of his supporters to "keep the pressure on," Senator Obama was successful in the historic election, in which people's emotions ran high and they were overly anxious that things were going to change dramatically. Many thought, we will now have a leader with good judgment, very intelligent, possess an ability to rally the nation behind him and displays thoughtful analyses of the important issues. The Alaska *Daily News*, hometown paper of Governor Sarah Palin, endorsed Senator Obama stating, he "brings far more promise to the office. In a time of grave economic crisis, he displays thoughtful analysis, enlists wise counsel and operates with a cool, steady hand." And further, he possesses good "judgment to shape a solution, as well as the leadership to rally the country behind it," the paper said.

These then were some of the issues that attracted and kept interested a great many people who worked for him, prayed for him, and voted for him, as Senator Barack Hussein Obama rose from relative obscurity to become a household-word worldwide. Even more important, he proved to be a terrific role model for many, black and white, men and women, old and young and even more significant he will change the world's opinion of America. He's been described as a terrific dad and an exceptional family man. Have you seen the picture of him washing the dishes in the kitchen! Equally significant, he particularly made African Americans proud. One tearful black woman, after Senator Obama's victory said she was "Proud to be black! Proud to be American!" As Colin Powell said, "He's won! It's over!" Thank you, President-elect Barack Hussein Obama.

("Barack Obama: Road to the White House" New York *Daily Challenge* Newspaper, November 13, 2008, pp. 4-5.

Senator Obama Addresses the Black Caucus
Foundation, Inc. Photo by B. Twilly.

Which Way America?

By Dr. Fred Monderson

Now that the nominees of the two major political parties, Democratic and Republican, Obama and McCain, have been more or less chosen, the still more difficult part of the presidential election of 2008 begins in earnest. The two candidates must marshal their ideas, positions and platforms; their supporters and political bases; fundraisers and appeal at their respective political conventions; to be chosen as standard bearers or leaders of their individual parties, all by the end of the summer. From Labor Day to the National Election day, the first Tuesday in November, the sprint is thus on to convince the majority of savvy American voters, that either Obama or McCain is the most viable and sincere leader to head the nation at this; perilous, time in its history. That individual must demonstrate he can be an effective chief executive, Commander-in-Chief, Head of State and possess the presidential timber to also be leader of the free world, more so than did President Bush, and his Vice-President Chaney, who have had such difficulties. That individual must also present clear and new policies that reflect a profound sense of visionary leadership that prepares Americans for the future, with change in many crucial areas of this democracy.

Just as the primaries featured many firsts in terms of personalities who ran, the general election can also boast of a somewhat similar distinction. John McCain, the Arizona Senator, a respected and honored veteran of Vietnam with tremendous Washington experience and political connection; is pitted against a somewhat inexperienced Barack Obama, a first-term Senator from Illinois, whose meteoric rise to national prominence is nothing short of phenomenal.

Despite claims of maverick independence, by virtue of being Republican, McCain is saddled with the albatross of President Bush's failed domestic, foreign, and particularly economic policies, that have run the economy aground with high unemployment; an economic recession that numbers high foreclosure rates, rising costs for food and fuel; absence of universal health care coverage; many children left behind; an exorbitant national debt; and a weakened dollar abroad. While an unpopular war has scarred the president's legacy, the one bright spot in his tenure is the prevention of another terrorist attack on American soil. However and whereas, in the past republicans have amplified America's fears, *a la Willie Horton* with Michael Dukakis and the *Swift-boat* attacks on John Kerry's Vietnam service credibility, and terrorist threats to the nation; at this juncture, however, the people have become wise to the machinations of the "Carl Rove political strategy playbook." This, then, is the legacy that President Bush bequeaths the Republican Candidate John McCain, and now the senator must distance himself from this and rise above, while convincing the people he can change the culture of Washington, and bring about the requisite reforms sorely needed today.

Obama, on the other hand, untainted by lengthy Washington residence, head of the "hungry democrats," heir to the perennial cycle of "throwing out the bums," proponent of a new philosophy of change is determined to phase out "business as usual" in Washington; and restore the prestige, respect, moral authority and American leadership in the world. To accomplish this, he must mobilize his base particularly among young people, and especially blacks, and win over portions of Hillary's disaffected supporters, win over many more independents, form a coalition between Hispanics, Native Americans, Catholics, gays, lesbians, physically challenged, white men, working people, then exhibit a greater appeal to women and make inroads among the Republicans who are more pro American than their party's recent, ethical and moral legacy indicates. While these are attainable goals,

Obama must also continue to appeal to first time and more educated voters, register more new voters, work for a greater turnout, while staying above the fray and minimizing his errors, keeping close tabs on party volunteers, deflecting the media's criticism, staying focused and smiling, even on "rainy days."

All this is not a means to an end, for after being elected President of the United States; the difficult journey begins, since he must now implement the campaign pledges, platform and promises. Many "eyes will be focused on Obama," scrutinizing his domestic, foreign, media and military positions and policies, and this includes terrorists, well wishers and adversaries alike. Therefore, what Obama does next to accomplish, if at all possible, nearly 100 percent of the things mentioned and then some, has to be looked for in examples from history. After all, Malcolm X once said, "History is a good teacher." Dr. John H. Clarke of Hunter College, CUNY, also added, "History is a roadmap that tells where you have been, where you are and where you are heading." Perhaps, if we look at different administrations at the start of the 19th, 20th, and 21st Centuries, we can learn from their strategies, developments, policy implementation and outcomes.

In 1809, at the start of the 19th Century, James Madison succeeded Thomas Jefferson who served two terms in the young nation's history. In 1800, the population numbered 5 million. Jefferson had opposed the Federalists, favored limited decentralized government and made the Louisiana Purchase, doubling the size of the emerging nation. He also opposed the Alien and Sedition Acts, which had to do with the issue of immigration in his time. Tensions were brewing with Britain, and soon the nation was embroiled in the War of 1812, or "second war of independence," because Madison offered poor leadership on this conflict. And, so the war lasted until 1815, with Jackson as a local hero at the Battle of New Orleans. At that time France proved our staunchest ally. Still, Madison had help author the "Virginia Plan," and so was called the "Father of the Constitution." He wrote many of the Federal Papers and also proposed the Bill of Rights to Congress. In this period, the nation's economy was young, policies under Alexander Hamilton, the first Secretary of the Treasury, were just beginning to bear fruit, though Jefferson opposed many ideas of his financial plan.

Trade was increasing and the Industrial Revolution was dawning in these United States.

The slave system predominated in the agricultural south and light industry and manufacturing predominated in the north in what became the sectional division of the nation's economy. While Washington's Farewell Address had suggested a policy of neutrality in foreign relations, which led in turn to isolationism; America still chose to be friendly with all nations, while also planning a surprise party for the Barbary Pirates of North Africa. On humanitarian grounds, some say economic, the American Slave Trade was abolished in 1808, following the British Abolition of the trade in 1807. Nevertheless, the slave trade remained illegally practiced and in addition, the Internal Slave Trade developed with the most horrendous ramifications for the African woman, the notion of the black family, with long lasting psychological, emotional and social consequences for this group, and with setbacks for the abolitionist movement. Notwithstanding, the climate fostered subsequent focus on reform in America, while the nation also addressed internal improvements and inward and later westward expansion.

Call it, "growing pains," but as the 19th Century, called the "century of production," unfolded, cotton became king. General Jackson led a raid on the Florida Seminoles in 1818, President Monroe issued the Monroe Doctrine and there was Gabriel Prosser's rebellion. David Walker made his "Appeal" at a time contemporary with issues of the national bank and with 1832 South Carolina Nullification and threats of secession. Meanwhile in 1831, Nat Turner plotted and executed his rebellion. In the 1840's there was a war with Mexico in which Samuel Carson; the "runaway," was killed. Patterning the international or British abolitionist movement, men and women of goodwill worked for the abolition of slavery, prison reform, reform or debtor relief, women's rights, and rights of the insane. The Dred Scott's dilemma, John Brown's raid on Harper's ferry, the Lincoln-Douglas Debates, and the "House Divided" speech that was precursor to the catastrophic Civil War (1860-1865) which saw Lincoln's Abolition of Slavery, the Radical Republicans and the Civil War's 13th, 14th, 15th, Amendments were significant developments in the growing nation. As the nation expanded westward under Manifest Destiny, the nation's railways settled the west and military and civilian elements decimated and confined the Native Americans. Finally, Reconstruction, *Plessy v. Ferguson* (1896) and ultimately the Spanish American War were some of the principal issues and events that set the stage for the 20th Century further entrenchment of Republican power in the economic and political process of the nation's forward thrust.

While W.E.B. DuBois was quick to recognize the problem of the 20th Century would be "the color bar," in that era, Teddy Roosevelt characterized America's strength and power as "little carrot" and "big stick." By 1900, the American population had risen to 76 million persons and there were 3.1 million persons over age 65. In his 1903 *Corollary to the Monroe Doctrine* he flexed American muscle in domination of the Caribbean and Latin America areas through military intervention and regulations, as well as check on European interests in this New World area. He invaded Haiti, Honduras, the Dominican Republic and Nicaragua to show America's might. While Al Gore later boasted he "Created the Internet," Teddy Roosevelt arranged the Hay-Pauncefote Treaty and he also demarcated and built the Panama Canal by fostering revolution in Panama to secede from Columbia.

This governor from New York, in office 1901-1909, characterized his program as the "Square Deal," but he was known as the trustbuster, a conservationist, reformer and nationalist who led the "Charge up San Juan Hill," in the Spanish American War. He was followed by one term "dollar diplomacy" William Howard Taft who in turn was succeeded by Woodrow Wilson offering "moral diplomacy" as part of the progressive movement. In his tenure, the 16th Amendment in 1913 established the federal government's power to levy taxes on personal income. The 17th Amendment, also in 1913, allowed for people's direct election of Federal Senators.

As these issues began to unfold, Europe became unsettled by rapid growth, technological and industrial expansion, and domination of the world's peoples. Soon the ills of imperialism, nationalism, and militarism sounded the bells of war and threatened American isolationism.

American involvement in World War I with Wilson as President and his famous "14 Points" at the Paris Peace Conference; emergence of Marcus Garvey and the Universal Negro Improvement Association; the

1920s economic boom; the Harlem Renaissance; and the Stock Market Crash; all marked a turning point in American history. Issuance of the Stimson Doctrine against Japanese imperialism; wholesale desertion of the Republican Party by blacks in the 1932 election and Roosevelt's resulting New Deal; World War II; the Truman Doctrine; Korean War; and *Brown V. Board of Education of Topeka Kansas;* all set the stage for the Civil Rights Movement. The Assassination of John F. Kennedy; Vietnam and domestic protest against the war; and the deaths of Malcolm X, Martin Luther King and Bobby Kennedy marked a low point in American history and conscience. Nixon's opening to China and Russia; the rise and demise of the Black Panthers; Nixon's fall, Ford, and the Carter's Doctrine of "no negotiation with terrorists;" was followed by Ronald Reagan's "Build up to build down." Reagan gave us the Contras; invasion of Grenada; and union busting. In combination, the First Gulf War under George Bush's father; two Bill Clinton administrations; the Oklahoma Bombing; and then George W. Bush's two terms; all placed America in a downward spiral. Still, the American population had risen to more than 280 million by the year 2000, with 25 million persons over age 65.

September 11, 2001 was a turning point. All America's defenses were designed to face an outward threat. Never once did the nation think of an internal catastrophe with such far reaching ramifications, that is, despite the lessons of Oklahoma. The nation was united against Al Qaeda in Afghanistan; yet, divided against the invasion of Iraq with its resultant bleeding of the domestic agenda. The cost to underwrite an unpopular war and the impact of a global resentment against what was perceived as the arrogance of ugly Americanism tarnished this nation's image at home and abroad.

While we were sidetracked, Fareed Zakharia depicted "The Rise of the Rest." Some have argued, to extricate ourselves from the economic, military, diplomatic and scientific quagmire we now find ourselves in, will require severe belt tightening, conservation, national reconciliation and uniting the country for the betterment of all; as well as new and bold visionary thinking, sturdy leadership, and meaningful policies and execution are what's needed right now. Therefore, on that day on January 20, 2009, after Barack Obama takes the Oath of Office of President of the United States, one has to wonder if Justice Clarence Thomas will do the honors. Still, the new president has to hit the ground running.

The first period saw significant attention to internal improvements in such areas as roads, railways, manufacturing, industry, workers' rights, agriculture and trade. The second period equally focused great attention to health standards in factories and manufacturing, cities and domestic housing, railroad expansion, the way west, war with the Native Americans, emergence of trusts, corporations, banking and American foreign policy, closer scrutiny of the economy, programs to put the nation back to work and the expansion of industrial and military capacity. All this signaled the coming of age of the nation.

Now, in this third period, two Bush-Cheney terms have placed America in a rather precarious position, both at home and abroad. Change is in dire need and this is what the Democratic Candidate promises. Therefore, when elected President, Barack Obama has to address poverty in this rich nation; and by extension poverty abroad, within the realms of our allies and also among our adversaries, since this devastation must also be addressed, to help change our image in the minds of people. He must devote significant attention to internal improvements since America's bridges, roads, tunnels, and other transportation avenues are in dire need of repairs; so too the levees, for these are also sure ways to get the nation back to work. Change must address these issues. The housing industry is bleeding profusely, whether in foreclosures, problems in the mortgage market, rising rents particularly in urban centers, the cost of food and the need for constructing more low cost housing is critical. Unemployment is high, and these numbers certainly undercounts male blacks whose numbers are many times that of whites, in national reckoning. Many Americans lament the loss of leisure time to hold 2 and 3 jobs just to make ends meet. Yet, job creation should be rewarded and those corporations that outsource American jobs should be denied special privileges. Here again change is sorely needed. Opportunities for all to attend college should be foremost in the reckoning. The price of food continues to rise as the cost of fuel has skyrocketed, but we must also pay attention to food safety, and hire more inspectors to do a good job.

The nation must continue to fund research and development in the critical areas of alternative sources of energy, in medical treatment, scientific exploration and also work on conservation and environmental issues, while holding to high moral standards. As an immigrant nation we must have significant immigration reform. We must address issues of Native Americans. Global warming and development of alternative fuels are also significant issues the new president must address. Equally, the military budget should not and cannot, at this time, get smaller, since terrorists and other adversaries continue to be emboldened as we meet their challenges. Veterans should get their fair share in school and medical entitlements. The tax code must be reformed. We must continue to stand firmly with Israel but also insist that "settlements" undermine any peace effort. Schools are in great need of repair. Funding for expanded programs such as after school and pre-Kindergarten training, and payments to teachers are imperatives, so that we can compete globally in science, mathematics, social sciences and certainly in technical areas, which in today's world are front burner issues.

Racism, institutional and otherwise, racial profiling, police brutality, continued attention to the needs of the handicap, prison reform, crime, homelessness, transportation, women's right and serious consideration should be given for sexual preferences of individuals, which would also reflect a nation's intellectual, moral and ethical advancement in today's world. These things reinvigorate democratic practices and send meaningful messages abroad. Supreme Court appointments will shape the nation's legal conscience for decades to come and vacancies will deserve serious consideration. FEMA has to be revamped to meet domestic emergencies and another "Katrina" should not be permitted. Naturally, those victims of Katrina should be helped since many still languish from their horrific experiences. These, then, are some of the problems and issues that would be challenges the next president; more likely, Barack Obama, must face to take the high moral road and restore confidence in, as Al Gore said, "the high value of American democracy." Once changes establish the new direction for America, the world will see the evil of terrorism and unite and vanquish that specter that respects neither nation, man, woman or child.

("Which Way America?" New York *Daily Challenge* Newspaper Monday, June 30, 2008, pp. 4-5)

Obama: The Pragmatic Patriot

By Dr. Fred Monderson

Dr. Leonard James, Professor Emeritus of New York City Technical College of the City University of New York, for the longest taught his students, the three characteristics that govern the survival of any animal in a given environment are move, adapt or die. While Barack Obama will not move or die, he is fast becoming a pragmatist with great potential to adapt. He should and must recognize its time for America to gird itself in 'Jacob's coat of many colors" and face the future with a united front that seeks to "raise all boats" of the "America Armada." After all, it's time for America to recognize, reach into and draw upon its inner strength of the totality of its human and material resources.

While Barack Obama has a new vision for America, he is equally constrained by the dynamics of past history. As President of the United States, Commander-in-Chief and Chief Executive, the most important arsenal at his command is the national budget. In control of this financial behemoth, the president actually has a very limited wiggle room because many facets of the budget are, seeming beyond his control in terms of rights and responsibilities. Naturally, he can do a little trimming here and there, but the cuts can only appear superficial. The budget essentially consists of federal wages, entitlements, defense spending, grants and funding for various government departments. Less than 15% of the budget is therefore under the control of the president in which he can dole out favors to exert influence on significant groups.

Not to discount the power of the president by his "limitations in the budget," the Presidency of the United States is a very powerful institution, and the individual in occupancy wields enormous power since he leads a nation approaching 300 million persons. As such, the power of the next president, if it's the Democrat Barack Obama, has to manifest in domestic and foreign arenas. In both areas, President Bush was a failure. Now, however, as Head of State, President Barack Obama must repair and reestablish America's moral leadership at home and abroad. On a sliding scale, he must reconnect with our traditional and most favored allies. He must visit their capitals so their people can have visible evidence of his presence. He must do all things visiting heads of states do abroad: address the nation through its parliament, shake hands, kiss babies, accept bouquets, pose for photographs, visit historic sites, hold press conferences, go to church, if he's there on Sunday, meet with business leaders, and host a reception for his nationals and diplomatic personnel abroad. Having visited some of the greater allies, depending on his time abroad, then he must repeat the process among the lesser allies. That is the nature of superpower relationships.

With adequate preparation for the rookie president traveling abroad, the orchestrated press coverage, both domestic and foreign, upon his arrival back home; tired, but now wide eyed as a foreign policy/relations "expert," he gets the "rock star" treatment. Next begins the most difficult part of his tenure as president, as he seeks to address the concerns of the nearly 150 million citizens who voted for and against him.

As Chief Executive the president must focus on a legislative agenda that addresses the bread and butter issues of the American people, the economy, that is. He must work with the Congress, with his party, reach across the proverbial aisle to avoid gridlock, reach consensus and expedite legislation that addresses first economic issues. High on this agenda must be the looming recession and need to jump start the economy by addressing infrastructure considerations as bridges, tunnels, roads, ports, transportation avenues, and housing construction and foreclosures. In addition, tax reform is important, overhaul of the banking system with emphasis on deposit requirements to avoid bank collapse; the FDIC and equally the Federal Reserve System to establish more efficiency in the oversight of the national economy are priority issues for the president.

To the extent that all boats are not raised at once, unemployment insurance must be extended, the "safety net" of food stamps and other subsidies for the poor must be continued and the national question of health care must be resolved. Immigration reform must remain a front burner issue with the need to expedite processing of legal applications and giving consideration to those whose status is in limbo.

Global warming, the environment, energy independence and alternative sources of energy as well as endangered species of flora and fauna must get immediate attention. More adequate preparation must be provided to address national emergencies with more urgency; greater emphasis must be made to strengthen and give priority to education preparation in terms of instruction, materials, and competitiveness. Research and development must be adequately funded to restore America's scientific leadership in the world and to continue outer and inner space exploration. He must seek to balance the budget and address trade imbalance. The minimum wage must keep pace with inflation. And he must insist the major auto makers produce cars with better gas mileage and strive for higher vehicular emission standards. The president must form a consensus to make permanent the Voting Rights Act that presently must be renewed every 25 years. Serious consideration must be given to statehood for the District of Columbia. He must wage a more credible war on drugs and seriously address the "Palestinian Question."

As Commander-in-Chief, President Obama must address the state of readiness of the armed forces, particularly in these trying times of terrorism and threats to the national interest. Personnel and material resources must remain sufficiently adequate to deter threats and to provide adequate medical and compensatory entitlements to active duty servicemen and veterans "who have borne the battle of service." As an adjunct to military effectiveness, coordination with Homeland Security Administration, and other domestic and foreign intelligence agencies must be more resolutely pursued to deter threats as far as possible to the nation. While the president has chosen to speak with our adversaries, he must show American resolve and carry the stick too.

Another of the "hats" the president wears is that of party leader and President Obama must heal any and all rifts within the Democratic Party. He must not be afraid to entertain Republican ideas and reach across the aisle in the national interest. Also, as Chief Fundraiser for the Democratic Party, the president must enrich the party's national, state and local coffers, then provide enough moral and material suasion to help put democrats in elected legislative positions. From the "grassroots" on up, everyone must benefit from the referent power of the president.

Therefore, with his domestic agenda set, the military adequately provided for, his party enjoying a relieved popularity, the president can now, with the new state of leadership, turn to judicial appointments at the supreme, appeals and circuit courts levels of administration. With the nation's confidence restored, the new style of leadership and with the party in control of the legislature, his Supreme Court appointments can be more readily accepted and pushed through the legislative process.

While the "honeymoon" or transition will be over within 60 days, assessment begins to be made after the first 90 days. Still, at the end of the first year, with the president firmly seated in the saddle, many of the earmarked agenda items principally, addressed, if not, accomplished as he heads towards the halfway point in his first administration, he can venture abroad with all of the indictors, viz., economic, trade, military, scientific research, environmental, educational, etc., all showing positive signs, he can now speak and act with greater authority, as leader of the west.

As much as the remnants of the "axis of evil," "global bad boys," and terrorists were given the requisite attention, he can now more meaningfully "full-court press" them and have his allies gladly fall in line in this respect. Thus, with "all his dogs barking" at the "big money items," he should more meaningfully address mundane issues as homophobia, women's right to choose, school prayer, racial profiling, racism, police brutality, the rights of the handicap, prison reform, the scourge of drug proliferation in the minority communities, high black and other ethnic unemployment, job training, the issue of illegal guns in poor communities and the stigma of same sex relationships.

All things being equal, many of his campaign promises kept, Barack Obama can begin to plan for his re-election, that elite club of great presidents who are twice elected, rule well, and with a minimal history of scandals.

In preparation for his exit from the two term presidential stage, the president must consider, in his right to pardon, not simply those with wealthy connections, but individuals who have served credible time in prison for crimes that can be forgiven. There are many political prisoners in America who have served countless years for grievances that were grounded in social inequities. Let's face it, the Russians threatened to annihilate us with their nuclear power. Today we are friends and they have favored nation status. The same goes for China. Within the past decade much has been said about the "axis of evil," yet we can "forgive" them. After all, despite what's been said about Iran, under the Bush Administration, we supply them with more goods, in trade.

So political prisoners have committed a crime against the state, they have served lengthy time, now show some compassion and pardon them. Men have committed more egregious crimes; some have stolen millions of dollars and gotten away with a slap on the wrist or little or no time in prison. The legislature should also be mindful that ex-offenders have served them time in prison, should have the basic and fundamental right of Americans to vote, restored to them. This form of state sponsored terrorism of dis-franchising ex-cons, particularly as it targets blacks, should be outlawed. Let's remember, as we preach morality abroad, our house could use a little housecleaning. ("Obama: The Pragmatic Patriot" New York *Daily Challenge* Newspaper, Tuesday August 12, 2008, pp. 4-5.

"ALL THE MARBLES."

BY DR. FRED MONDERSON

The big showdown at the Democratic National Convention has more long lasting implications than the casual observer can easily discern. While the whole world will be watching, some of us will also be doing the same thing.

On August 13, 2008, Fox News, aired on a Guyanese television, showed the leader of a disaffected movement of the failed Presidential Nomination bid of Senator Hillary Rodham Clinton, who unequivocally boasted "If Hillary is not on the ticket, many of us are voting for McCain!" The gall of this pseudo-Democrat whose "sour-grapes" attitude is reminiscent of the "Creole" saying, he wants to "cut his nose to spite his face." Well, what type of message is this fellow and his group sending to blacks and other ethnicities that loyally support the Democratic Party?

In the run-up to the 2006 Congressional Elections, Harry Belafonte, Dr. Leonard James, and I took a position that for black people, especially, a democratic victory is infinitesimally small, policy wise, when compared with the Republicans, who have ignored this important constituency for the longest time. The democrats need remember in the 1932 National Elections, because of the policy of ignoring them; blacks bolted the Republican Party enmasse, remaining faithfully democratic since.

Those who forget history are bound to repeat its mistakes. Those who ignore examples are sometimes victims in the same manner. Therefore, when playing for "All the Marbles," all the players need consider the variety of options and their potential for execution. If those players of "Russian Roulette," want to commit "Hari Kari," their bluff can easily be called. Importantly, however, their platform mantra for such blatant betrayal, that Obama is "only the presumptive democratic nominee" in view of Senator Hillary Clinton's failure to acquire such a status, may not be the full story behind their treacherous revolt.

Such a claim as Obama is "not ready to lead," "inexperience in the domestic and international political arenas," and his "flip flop" on various positions are all founded on spurious and faulty reasoning. While we cannot dismiss the gains made by minorities in America; race has always been a factor when it involves blacks whether in politics, economic progress and educational and intellectual advancement in this nation. Notwithstanding, history is replete with examples of instances where, when obstacles are removed, then blacks can and do excel in positions of leadership, whether in the private or public sector of administration.

As a free and independent thinker, while its near the Convention, and some ten weeks before the National Elections, and before I call for blacks to bolt the Democratic Party, if given this, then that; let me assess some of the contemporary issues, and those that will have a bearing on policy and response responsibilities of the next President of the United States.

Emeritus Professor Leonard James of the African American Studies Department of New York City Technical College, of CUNY, always taught that there are internal and external factors, which he called *causes stimuli* that influence the rise, development and decline of states. This concept can also be applied to individual persons who are in positions of importance and whose thinking has a bearing on developments that affect a great many people. Therefore, the recent events involving Russia is a good example of an external happening that has a bearing not simply on American response to this development, but also affects the internal position and responses of the presidential contenders.

I should point out; both McCain and Obama are in the same position of being "presumptive nominees" of their parties, on the eve of their Nominating Conventions. However, while no one has underscored that McCain is the "presumptive nominee" of the Republican Party; the "rebels" who intend to disrupt a *fail accompli* at the Democratic National Convention, constantly reminds us, Obama is just the "presumptive nominee." Importantly, while they do have a right to stage a "floor fight," such an action flies in the face of reason and defies all logic. Therefore, does the term "presumptive nominee" mean two different things to two different parties? Or, do these agenda people have "an axe to grind."

Nevertheless, and first, the Russian invasion of the territory of the sovereign nation of Georgia is one instance of how, unexpectedly, challenges can appear on the landscape that threatens or challenges the national interest. Equally, leadership response in each situation varies but also is an indicator or barometer of how well the more pressing ones are dwelt with. Even more important, since nothing is written in stone, in today's state of affairs, noting can be taken for granted, anyone and everything is suspect, and only after the fat lady has sung, can we get a clear understanding of things.

The media was quick to point out, while President Bush sat with Russian Prime Minister Putin, enjoying the Olympics, probably sharing a brew, a few slaps on the back, and exchanging pleasantries of "Barber shop chit chat," Kremlin tanks rolled into Georgia. Obviously, even though President Bush was able to "look deep into Putin's soul," he was still surprised by this recent military deployment sleight of hand. Some have argued it was the Georgian President who forced the issue in his view, at an opportune time. Quite obviously, he never envisioned a Russian response of the magnitude that transpired. Still others have argued the whole episode was orchestrated so that John McCain could be elected along a line that he is tough. This take, however, is near sighted and riddled with flaws, for a number of reasons.

First of all, the Presidential or National Elections in this country is more than ten weeks away and a great many developments can transpire before then. For instance, a good example is the rapidity with which France and Russia were able to hammer out a peace agreement, despite the fact it may be broken and hostilities are continuing. A skirmish of this nature has the potential to spread beyond the current border and no one wants a war in Europe.

For years, untold numbers have argued and labeled President Bush a war monger. His quick response of dispatching humanitarian aid to Georgia, using military transport, however, is timely, yet, with the potential for escalation in a number of ways. Such an act does give him credit for being decisive, on the one hand, while on the other, claims were made that Senator McCain had pointed to this potential development nearly two years ago. It could equally be argued, his seniority and intelligence connections in Congress could have rightly identified this potentially explosive situation and he passed it on.

In this situation, the theory of experience is put to the test, for, though President Bush has enjoyed two terms in his position, yet, distracted by the albatross of Iraq, he was blindsided by this challenge. This could be one example that experience is not always the best teacher.

Naturally, in this as in any newsworthy issue, the presidential candidates John McCain and Barack Obama were questioned and their responses noted.

John McCain stated pointedly, "The Russians should stand down!" Barack Obama, on the other hand, explained he "consulted with Secretary of State Condoleezza Rice and a number of other significant minds" and expressed the view, "This issue should be resolved through negotiations." These two positions go a long was in characterizing the two candidates. Despite the fact, McCain is not the President and cannot seek to confront the Russians. That is George Bush's job. McCain then is disposed to "Shoot first, talk later!" Is this a manifestation of "Bush Three?" Remember what happened to Al Haig when President Reagan was shot. He said: "I'm in charge." In fact, the Vice-President, then the speaker came before him. However, we understood he simply wanted to let adversaries know and reassure the American people, someone was still watching the store, while the leader was fallen. Still, he was fired for "insubordination."

Notwithstanding, despite claims he is inexperienced, Obama demonstrated the more circumspect position in keeping with his stated desire to talk first. After all, let's say, for argument sake, the Russians responded arrogantly to the "McCain position," then we would be seriously challenged in a military confrontation in Georgia. "The American people," even as General George Patton liked to say, "love a good fight." But battle scarred, war weary and over-extended in Iraq and Afghanistan, with Iran looming on the horizon, the American people may be reluctantly pulled into a major confrontation, something they do not desire at this time. Therefore, such a major blunder by McCain should put the nation on guard. Equally, this response seems as flawed as Senator Clinton's outspoken intent to "nuke Iran," if it harms Israel!

While we're committed to Israel's defense, unequivocal threats to bomb before negotiation, is clearly brash and cannot be the first option by any American administration in this new age. Besides, when we keep our adversaries guessing as to our actions, we're better able to deploy the most feasible course of action, whether its economic sanctions, diplomatic pressures, and only as a last resort, the threat of military action in a big way.

The question, then, is whether the "Hillary miscreant movement" is really prepared, if the Senator is not on the ballot, "to give it to McCain." Clearly then, unmasked, while their option is not sound, then there may be more to their course of action. Therefore, it's a valid question to all, whether this position is fueled by racial considerations and should we allow them to poison the American voting pool.

Equally, even if Obama "flip flops" on any of the issues pressing the American people, whether it's the economy, a sound energy policy, food prices, the looming recession, and so on, it is based on his consultation with that great reservoir of American expertise, the "Think tank," that allows his final position to be rooted in consensus thinking that shapes his final determination. In that reaching out approach, he seems to have found favorable reception in the likes of Colin Powel, for there is talk, the former Secretary of State plans to endorse Obama. Chuck Hegel, some of the generals and naturally his democratic heavy hitters such as Ted Kennedy, Bill Richardson and Gov. Warner, are indications

Obama is "doing the right thing." Even New York City's Mayor Mike Bloomberg, in his Florida statement regarding Obama's support of Israel, indicated the man knows what he is doing and spurious claims regarding his questionable intent must be dismissed as false rumors designed to mislead. Therefore, Obama's choice as the democratic standard bearer in the November general elections should not be side tracked. ("All the Marbles" New York *Daily Challenge* Newspaper, Wednesday August 20, 2008, pp. 4-5)

OH,
JOHN, NO!

BY DR. FRED MONDERSON

Clearly, a sign of a faltering, fading political campaign is a move off the dime of substantive issues and attack one's opponent using the *Ad Hominem* or throw mud argument or strategy. This is what John McCain's "attack dog," the "pit bull in lipstick," "won't answer the questions" Governor Sarah Palin, did this week past.

While Sarah Palin, the Republican party's candidate for Vice-President, in the recently concluded Vice-Presidential Debate with Joe Biden, kept accusing Barack Obama, the democratic standard bearer, of looking to the past, proclaiming their candidacy is focused on the future; she fired a "low ball" at Obama, accusing him of associating with "terrorists," In fact, the 1960's radical George Ayers of the Weather Underground, is today a respected Professor at an Illinois University, and Obama is or was not that close to Ayers. Some believe the "terrorist" claim is a stretch to imply association of such behavior with Muslims. This brings us to the circular and false charge that "Obama is a Muslim." Therefore "barracuda" Sarah's charge is actually a rehashing of the past.

No one can doubt McCain served his country in Vietnam and was proclaimed a hero! He certainly got his recognition and this propelled him to national prominence in government and social circles. While this happened some 50 years ago, he has certainly "milked it" for decades.

Imagine, for nearly 50 years, so many times per year, everywhere, John McCain, HERO! So much so, today it's still on the lips of veterans, non-veterans, the candidates, the media, etc. What about those of us who served in that war, who got no recognition; called baby killers; pestered for fighting an unjust war; ridiculed; put out to pasture before our time. The truth is that many of these veterans never recovered, becoming wasted through substance abuse, cascading into a downward spiral; many dead before age 50.

How about those of us who lost limbs, those who lost their minds, who were shot, who lost their lives, who still are haunted by the lost lives of friends and their experiences, who were forgotten for so many years; who never got a welcome home party! What about the black soldiers who got Bronze Star medals instead of Silver Stars for bravery and heroism? Even today, many Vietnam veterans languish, are unemployed, unemployable, homeless, sleeping in the streets, in parks, hostels, homeless shelters, many who are forgotten and some are now finally getting "some recognition" some 50 years later. So, unlike John McCain who enjoyed almost 50 years of recognition and accolades, praise should also go out to those "modern foot soldiers" who are now helping veterans get some of what they rightly deserve.

Governor Palin's accusation against Senator Barack Obama is certainly an appeal to the past rather that to the future. Therefore, this and so many of their strategies are clearly false acts of disrespect and desperation, particularly in view of the recent polls showing Obama ahead in many key states once considered Republican or toss-up. What is significant, many such charges were leveled in the Democratic Primary and still the American people voted Barack Obama that party's standard bearer. What's even more important are the ongoing character, and other forms of assassination Barack Obama has been exposed to. For example, the media reported the FBI was investigating "men with guns" in Obama's vicinity. He was accused of being inexperienced. Obama was accused of taking money from the Freddie Mac and Fannie Mae lobby, that so many politicians have similarly done to finance their re-election campaigns. Senator Obama was accused of wanting to sit down and negotiate with "international bad boys" from "pariah nations." Obama was accused of not serving in the military, yet he wants to be Commander-in-Chief. I don't think Abraham Lincoln served in the military! What about those Americans who "hid in colleges" and "ran away to Canada" while others served in Viet Nam. Today, some of these same people are in the highest echelons of the Fortune 500 business companies that significantly impact this country economically. Who knows, they may very well be Wall Street tycoons and banking leaders who are directly responsible for the current economic mess the country is now in.

Barack Obama's wife Michele was attacked as part of that "classic republican," a-la-"Carl Rove Play Book" and viz., "Willie Horton," and "Swift Boat," mentality that exposed a sinister side of the Republican Party. While Barack was accused of "lack of leadership skills," he certainly demonstrated forceful leadership when he responded to the attack on his wife by saying: "If you are listening, lay off my wife!" Guess what, Michele Obama was then spared this awfully shoddy political treatment.

When Russia invaded an American ally, Georgia, McCain rushed to tell the Russians they should "stand down!" Remember when President Reagan was shot by Hinckley, the then Secretary of State Al Haig, good intentioned as he was, in trying to warn the nation's enemies, that someone was at the wheel, said: "I'm in charge!" This was an inappropriate response because the Constitution says; the Vice-President and then Speaker of the House of Representatives are next in the chain of command. Haig was fired for overstepping his authority! Since McCain was nowhere in the hierarchy of succession and since it is President Bush who must speak for the nation on foreign affairs, then McCain was out of order for his "shoot from the hip," I mean lip, approach. On the other hand, Barack Obama, in true leadership style, consulted with some of the nation's leadership foreign policy and think tank members including Secretary of State Condoleezza Rice. He then issued a considered statement that the problem should be solved by negotiation. That is certainly thoughtful leadership not cowboy brinksmanship! Again, when the Wall Street mess broke, affecting AIG, Wachovia, Lehman Brothers, Bear Sterns, WaMu, etc., McCain instantly said "fire the FCC Chairman." Obama, on the other hand, again consulted with his business and economic leaders and was shown with them before he issued a well thought out response. Here again he demonstrated a cool and calculated leadership style that did not plunge the nation headlong into a mess, that had to be cleaned up a week later. Still more, with the "bailout bill," McCain suspended his campaign and rushed back to Washington but could not deliver the Republican votes in the House of Representatives to pass the measure. This haste played a big role in its failure despite the measure's distaste, while Obama went into consultation and caucusing on Capitol Hill, then his response was not as embarrassing as his opponent. Subsequently, the measure passed and both men helped this time in moving the bill forward.

Barack Obama was berated for being a Community Organizer, implying such employment is not worth the consideration and respect as representative of leadership qualities. That is, despite the successes community organizers accomplish in terms of helping community residents with their problems as these unfolded. How tragic! Tip O'Neal, the former Massachusetts Speaker of the House was credited with saying "All politics is local." This means politics or political or social organizing begins with the local level or from the bottom up. In political parlance, it's organizing from the home, block, precinct, election district, statewide, federal senate, national leadership; all that brings about the desired political election results. In some organizations one has to work one's way from the mailroom up to the presidency!

Another example can be gleaned from, for example, in New York City. The Mayor, City Council, Boro-Presidents, all undertake their respective functions. However, much of the coordinating of community day to day functions, viz., fire, parks and recreation, education, police, environment/sanitation, housing, aging, youth and family services, health, transportation, economic development, library, re: nuts and bolts issues that keeps the community functional by serving its needs of problem solving, is done at the Community Board level. This is as basic "grass roots" organizing as you can get, somewhat similar to Community Organizing. However, while the latter is semi-private, the former is quasi-governmental. Nevertheless, and importantly, Community Board members serve without pay and the Board employees get low pay!

In essence then, with her recent "terrorist" accusation, Governor Sarah Palin, and the much too "un-presidential" Senator McCain's approval, has thrown the "kitchen sink" to assassinate the character of Senator Barack Obama, but this too will fail! However, such an undertaking has truly exposed the "teeth" or fangs of the "Pit-bull" despite the camouflage of its "lipstick," so characteristic of "barracuda Sarah."

What Senator McCain and his surrogate, Governor Palin, have failed to recognize, such "terrorist" and "inexperienced" charges against Barack Obama have been dismissed by the American people who recognize they want leadership not "smoke and mirrors," and have dismissed such name calling as "electioneering politics."

Barack Obama has been accused of being a Muslim because of his name, given by his East African father. Barack has been accused of being unpatriotic and not having served in the military. Barack was accused of not wearing a pin of the flag on his lapel. He was accused of not remembering the name of the soldier, whose bracelet he is wearing. Senator Barack Obama was accused of being a celebrity. For forty years McCain has been celebrated as a Viet Nam war hero celebrity. Obama has been accused of being famous worldwide and needs to be President of the world, not the United States. He has been accused as not being ready to lead through inexperience.

Now, instead of the negative *Ad Hominem*, the McCain/Palin team should explain to the American people why in the month of September 2008, the nation lost more than 159,000 jobs and more than 700,000 jobs for the year of 2008. They should give a clear indication where they stand on that failure of the Bush Administration that is at the root cause of this problem. How will they remedy this and the need to create more meaningful jobs to stimulate the economy?

The McCain/Palin team should tell the American people why the Republican Party has allowed such rampant economic deregulation over much of the last dozen years when they controlled the Congress and White House. This has allowed banks and Wall Street CEOs to create a rather devastating impact on the nation's finances, fueling a recession taking its toll on citizens' pocketbooks.

The McCain/Palin team should clearly spell out how different their program for the future of the American nation is than that of the George Bush's administration, which has led the nation into its present economic quagmire. The McCain/Palin team must clearly spell out their immigration policy and health care initiatives.

The McCain/Palin team should explain to the American people why major corporations, who have gotten so much in tax breaks under the Bush administration, should continue to get additional billions in tax cuts, particularly in view of the current state of the national economy. They must give convincing arguments as to why should the Bush tax cuts should be continued?

The McCain/Palin team should explain what is their end-game strategy to clearly "close the book" on Iraq. They must equally state how they intend to deal with the Pakistan situation of nuclear technology and radical Islamic terrorism. They must be convincing about how they would deal with Afghanistan, and this strategy should not be conducted as has happened in Iraq. They should explain how they intend to capture Bin Laden, Al Zawahiri, and deal with Al Qaeda, since the present administration has not been successful in pursuit of any of these objectives.

The McCain/Palin team should reassure the American people they are not taking the "low road" to the highest office in the land, despite previous claims not to sink to this level. Is this flip-flop? They should promise the American people to not tell them Barack Obama is black! Everyone knows this.

The McCain/Palin team should inform the American people, since they intend to represent all Americans, what role will minorities play in their administration.

The McCain/Palin team should explain to the American people, whose husbands, wives, sons and daughters have served in Iraq and Afghanistan, what type of educational entitlement they will support as these veterans seek to readjust when they return from battle and then prepare for the future. They should also get some of the heroes' treatment McCain has enjoyed for nearly 50 years, because they too have served.

Having said all that, the McCain/Palin team must "Get out of the political gutter," and wage a credible and respectable campaign on the issues and not stoop to the art of character assassination. This turns off the astute and critical voter who is more interested in issues than character. By this I mean discuss programs that address "bread and butter" issues that concern the great majority of the American people, particularly those on "Main Street."

Someone, I think it was George Will, who said: "We do not elect an angry person President," and in this he meant John McCain is angry, and his campaign is faltering and thus, turning negative. As this is what the McCain campaign has promised for the last 4 weeks before the election. Then that's why Governor Sarah Palin has fired the first salvo across Barack Obama's bough. Of course, the shot fell short and exposed the desperate nature of the McCain/Palin presidential quest. No, John. No! BYE! BYE! ("Oh, John, No!" New York *Daily Challenge* Newspaper, October 9, 2008, pp. 4-5. 6)

OBAMA
THE VISIONARY

BY DR. FRED MONDERSON

Barack Obama, a state senator from Illinois, burst on the national scene at the 2004 Democratic National Convention with an outstanding keynote address that caused the nation to take notice of a young and upcoming leader with great potential. Within two years he was a U.S. Senator from his state and in four, after a testy democratic presidential primary in which he won 34 states, the democrats anointed him their standard bearer. Clearly, vision, fortitude, tenacity and a charismatic appeal propelled his meteoric rise in American and global politics and people prominence. When he appeared for political or other gatherings, Obama received "rock star" turnout and treatment. In this he surrounded himself with the best and brightest intellects, young and experienced thinkers and organizers.

For sure, *Fortuna* played a role in his unfolding phenomenon, but, let's not kid ourselves; there are more Obamas, black and white, men and women, out there. If only circumstances and luck would favor their exposure, perhaps this great nation could benefit enormously from their contributions. Notwithstanding, and without question, throughout the democratic primaries and now the presidential campaign, Obama has been accused, chided, in a word, belittled, as being nor ready to lead and being inexperienced or wallowing in Washington "taint." In fact, this latter is the least credible of all charges since his "recent arrival" in Washington precludes him from being awash in the grime of the capital, as so many who have been there for decades.

Possessing experience with the capacity to demonstrate decisive and correct judgment in any situation is not necessarily a given. Afterall, who had more experience in politics, government, the executive branch, than Vice-President Dick Chaney, and look how he helped muddle President George W. Bush's administrative policies with its devastating effect on the American body politic, economic functioning and infrastructure, the nation's image abroad and they have left a legacy, the subject of much discussion and analysis, for years to come. Therefore, experience is not always the best teacher or criteria for handling human affairs that can oftentimes be unpredictable. Afterall, folk wisdom teaches us, "You can find a man at 14 and a boy at 40." Look at Jesus, a 12-year old lad, befuddling the great minds of his day, and look at the impact he has had on subsequent civilization.

It was visionary thinking that Barack Obama, having "sowed his student oats" and at the crossroads of leaving Harvard University, armed with intellect and tenacity, the young attorney journeyed to Chicago to work as a Community Organizer. It was also visionary thinking when Barack set out from Columbia to Harvard and similarly, with his law degree, rather than Wall Street, he chose Main Street and thereabouts to work with and for the people.

There, in that cauldron of social inequity, amidst the trials and tribulations of the "grass roots," the pounding mettle was fired with the necessity of being an elected representative of the people to bring about the necessary change. Perhaps it was that great American, Malcolm X, who said "You want that great leader to bring change, look in the mirror." This is probably what first set Obama on that journey to government service. Certainly his visionary character and experiences gained in his Community Organizer role, enabled Barack to be successfully elected to the Illinois Senate and finally to its Federal Senate position. Again, it was Barack Obama's visionary character that then embarked him on the road to the White House. Who knows, perhaps he felt things were so bad then, he needed to step in as a change agent.

On the long road through the democratic primary and convention, Barack Obama, the first African American with a real shot at winning his party's nomination and ultimately the presidency, was the most seriously challenged of all candidates. By challenge, I do not mean the regular run of the mill such endeavors. The challenges Obama faced questioned his race, his patriotism, his religion, his experience and his leadership skills. They also questioned his social, religious and cultural associations, and his family, his wife Michele, that is, was equally subjected to unusual scrutiny, that was indeed unusual, compared with other candidates' wives.

A visionary characteristic is not an isolated trait, but perhaps it breeds a cool, considered and calculated demeanor that has allowed Barack to stay focused on task, deflect personal criticism, and still be able to deliver his message. Clearly, these traits were very evident to rational and well meaning individuals who soon recognized the significance of the moment when a visionary leader had appeared on the scene. Upon observation, his mannerism, and calm demeanor, soon fired their interest and people began to flock to his message of hope and change. This in turn motivated many others to register to vote and still others to volunteer their time to help his campaign. His confession that only a country like America could create, fuel and bring to fruition his story of rise from humble beginnings to aspiring to the highest office of the land was well received.

Those who followed the spirals of the democratic primary and presidential campaign are familiar with the numerous challenges Senator Obama faced in the hotly contested race to become his party's nominee. Concluding this quest, Obama's visionary outlook took him abroad first to Iraq, Afghanistan, the Middle East and then to Europe. In Iraq, the senator met with General Petraeus and Prime Minister Maliki; and got a tremendous grasp of the situation there. This first-hand briefing of the dynamics on the ground helped Obama see the true realities of the war, that as a visionary, he opposed from the beginning. Similarly, in Afghanistan, Senator Obama met with President Karzai and was made aware of the pitfalls, shortfalls and what needs to be done in the country that hopefully does not mirror Iraq's failed approach. In Europe his coming seemed proclaimed and was celebrated in a tumultuous manner seemingly by a people yearning to be shown a different path by Americans. That outstanding visionary characteristic enabled Senator Obama to recognize under the Bush Administration, America had alienated so many nations in the Western Alliance that there was need to reassure these allies change was coming and an Obama Administration intended to embark this nation on a new direction.

The tumultuous reception Senator Obama, the democratic party's then nominee for President of the United States, received in Europe was evident in that continent's yearning for change, better relations and the need for bold, decisive and visionary leadership in the alliance. Combining vision, confidence, and the now success of being chosen to lead the Democratic Party into the fall national elections, on that tour, Senator Barack Obama demonstrated outstanding diplomatic finesse, statesmanship, wherever he went, seemingly repairing the rifts that developed between his country and its friends and allies.

Barack Obama the visionary, particularly in view of today's global economic downturn, now in retrospect, anticipated this current quagmire and appropriately seems to have laid the groundwork for cementing better relationships between America and the west. Now poised for his biggest and most significant win, Obama may very well be the right prescription to move this country forward with the wherewithal to address the many domestic and international challenges facing his nation. A further aspect of his visionary character is Obama's ability to surround himself with think tank intellectuals and experts whose advice he listens to and has and will continue to enhance his leadership acumen.

An even more important hallmark of this visionary superman in the mix, is the rapid growth in Senator Obama's grasp of domestic and international political, economic, military and diplomatic realities in record time. Clearly his ability to conceptualize rapidly, readily and well has allowed Barack Obama to experience such phenomenal growth. During the primary debates Obama's competitors leveled the charge of his not being fit to lead. Interestingly enough, first Senator Joe Biden and then Senator Hillary Clinton constantly made this point questioning Barack's ability to lead. The results of the primary known,

Senator Obama chose Senator Biden to be his Vice-Presidential running mate. Instantly, immodest Biden was asked, 'Well, Senator, you leveled the charge Senator Obama was not experienced and so not qualified to lead, so why now having been chosen, you are prepared to follow him?' True to form, Biden confessed, Senator Obama has grown tremendously since that statement was first made more than a year ago, due to his exposures, challenges and successes in the primaries; his cool demeanor in times of challenges; his tour of Europe and the Middle East; his poise and diplomatic acumen; his rapid grasp of the issues, ability to communicate this; and his demonstration of what is considered "presidential timber."

What Senator Biden left out, or should I say, had not yet reached his desk, was the current Wall Street mess, involving Lehman Brothers, the American International Group (AIG), Bear Sterns, Wachovia, WaMu, the need for a federal 'bailout" or rescue, and the devastating impact of these factors on the American and global economic landscape.

The economic impact on Europe especially is reminiscent of Obama's early and visionary approach in reaching out to European nations, whose economies are now under enormous stress. Their anticipation of the American political change they could believe in, is now earnestly anticipated for these nations too believed, when Senator Obama reached across the oceans he was indeed a visionary they would like to work with. All that's left is for the American people to get on board and put Barack Obama, masterful visionary, to work to put his ideas into practice of bringing the people together, healing the nation and putting us in a forward looking path, that re-establishes America's leadership role in the world; some say the last hope for humanity!

("Obama the Visionary" New York *Daily Challenge* Newspaper, 2008, pp. 4-5)

Barack Obama: Ready, Fit To Lead

By Dr. Fred Monderson

Much has been said of Senator Barack Obama, but one thing is certain, he is a leader of extraordinary intellect, poise, skill, vision, charisma and prowess, as evidenced in his exceptional performance under media and public scrutiny in this 2008 political campaign. Having outdistanced and "lapped" his first round of opponents, he is now in the process of "walking away" from his current opponent, John McCain, as they both contend for the highest prize in the land, the Office of President of the United States of America. The wherewithal of this contest is the ultimate challenge that tests one's physical stamina, intellectual fortitude in generating and articulating ideas consistent with events and issues of the times, while motivating followers to remain focused on his message. This includes all the distractions opponents, their followers, proxies, and the media have a tendency to place in the path of a candidate of this nature.

When we turn to the great leaders of history, excepting generals, but men of ideas, action, who, called upon in times of crisis or serious challenge to a people, rose to the occasion and delivered hope and a message that provided vision and a way out of the troubles; such individuals only come in times, far and in-between.

In modern times such sterling character has been found in the person of Winston Churchill, Mahatma Gandhi, Eric Williams, Paul Robeson, W.E.B. DuBois, Marcus Garvey, Malcolm X, Martin Luther King, Jr., and John and Bobby Kennedy, and to this we can add Barack Obama, for he is certainly in the caliber of these great men of action, vision, fortitude and ideas that have stood the test of time. However, what makes Barack Obama even more special, though he follows in the footsteps of these men; is the humble beginnings from which his aspirations emerged along the arduous path to the biggest office of the land. The times and challenges of his era are different, more widespread, require greater input more readily. In many ways Barack Obama fits the mold of the quintessential leader amidst the nation's trials and tribulations; but he has also possessed the courage and conviction of answering the call and the ability to convincingly convey this to the people.

Leaders are not born; they are made, as a result of circumstances in which they find themselves. While military leaders are precluded from this experience, a military analogy is not inappropriate. Battlefield promotion or command is given in the thick of things, for while colleagues are falling left and right and the situation seems chaotic, an individual steps forward, brings order to havoc, provides leadership, direction, demonstrates courage and thereby gains the respect and support of those in the same quandary, they all find themselves in. Thereafter the superiors promote this individual because he has rescued the situation and demonstrated leadership.

While the ancient Chinese philosopher Lao-tzu in *The Way of Life* has held, "A leader is best when people barely know that he exists," and Havelock Ellis (1859-1939) in *Against the Grain* stated, "To be a leader of men one must turn one's back on men." However, rightly, none of these admonitions apply to Barack Obama. On the other hand, Nicolai Machiavelli (1469-1527) in *The Prince* believed, "There is nothing more difficult to take in hand, more perilous to conduct or more uncertain in its success, than to take the lead in the introduction of a new order of things." Interestingly, this latter seems more appropriate to Barack Obama's view of initiative and change. Again, William Bolitho in *A Memoir:* "Roosevelt has Gone" on April 14, 1945 wrote: "The final test of a leader is that he leaves behind him in other men the conviction and the will to carry on....The genius of a good leader is to leave behind him a situation which common sense, without the grace of genius, can deal with successfully." Two terms later, when President Obama makes way for his successor, the fundamental initiatives for change he effectuated would easily be continued and this is consistent with the latter description of the leader's efforts.

John Kennedy (1917-1963) that quintessential young President, in a television address on July 4, 1960, told the American people, in a lead-up to the national election: "It is time for a new generation of leadership, to cope with new problems and new opportunities. For there is a new world to be won." These sentiments fit Barack Obama to a "T." Afterall, Barack's is part of a new generation of leadership. The new problems of his era can be measured in the economic catastrophe facing the nation and world, fueled by the "mess on Wall Street." These problems in job loss; home foreclosures; need for meaningful healthcare changes; education demands in better instruction, teacher remuneration, and building improvement in physical structure and technical improvement in equipment and expertise; retirement concerns; energy independence and alternatives; the need for tax reforms; terrorist threats; wars in Iraq and Afghanistan; the challenge of nations seeking nuclear power for whatever reason; and America's crumbling bridge, road, and tunnel infrastructure in need of immediate repairs; are all problems that must be addressed by a new mindset of visionary thinking and bold leadership.

The new opportunities presented to Senator Barack Obama when he becomes President, is to let the American people signal to the world after the election, their intention to create new pathways for the nation to now embark. This will allow President Obama to repair relations with allies alienated by the Bush Administration's foreign policy arrogance and signal America's adversaries, while we're strong enough, secure enough to respond to your challenge, we're giving you a chance to sit down and discuss differences, before we resort to the full range of challenging options, viz., military, diplomatic, economic., etc., that can be exercised. As President, he must also move expeditiously to repair the fractured American system.

Again, John Kennedy in "Remarks prepared for delivery at the Trade Mart in Dallas," November 22, 1963, reminded all, "Leadership and learning are indispensible to each other." How appropriate is this admonition to Barack Obama's phenomenal growth as a leader. In the early phases of the Democratic Primary campaign Senator Joe Biden accused Barack Obama of not being ready or fit to lead. Obama's opponents grabbed the ball, I mean the idea, and carried it, seemingly forever. But, while these people were hung up on this line, Barack went to work, I mean, school, and shored up whatever weaknesses he may have had in this respect. Surrounding himself with some of the best economic, military and foreign policy minds in the nation, infusing his quick grasp of ideas, Obama then went abroad to acquire a better grasp of the situation in Iraq and Afghanistan. After, he moved on to Europe to see and be seen, meet and greet and add to his experience bank in diplomatic, foreign policy and people and cultural relations. In Europe, as is well known, he was well received as if signaling their desire for a change in relations with America.

So much so, nearly a year after beginning his presidential campaign quest he won the Democratic nomination and Senator Obama chose Senator Joe Biden to be his running mate. Instantly the media enquired, "Senator Biden, you first said Senator Obama was not ready to lead, and now chosen as his Vice-Presidential running mate, you are prepared to follow him. How is this?" To which Senator Biden replied, in essence, Senator Obama has learned a great deal from the time that was said to now. He has learned and demonstrated this to the millions who voted for him. He has learned much from his travels abroad. He has also learned a great deal from studying the blunders the Republicans have made in mismanaging the economy and foreign policy of this nation, over the last eight years. This then gives Senator Barack Obama high marks not only for his active mind, historical experience but also an ability to grasp an idea and run with it, much to the approval of his followers. Thus, President Kennedy's notion of leadership and learning appropriately applies to Senator Obama as this is his mantra!

Harry S. Truman (1884-1972), United States President, who succeeded Franklin D. Roosevelt, firmly believed, "A leader has to lead, or otherwise he has no business in politics." This is precisely what Barack

Obama has done in his meteoric rise from relatively obscurity to first win 34 states in the Democratic Presidential Primary and subsequently held his own, gaining respectable leads from state to state, or shrinking the lead of John McCain, who first ran for President in 2000 and now in 2008. Certainly Senator McCain is a seasoned campaigner, well known across "every nook and cranny" of this nation, and a heroic veteran of the Viet Nam war. Still, Barack Obama, according to the polls, is either beating Senator McCain or holding him at bay.

In a town hall meeting last week, many who turned out to greet Senator McCain were "angry" about his showing in the polls. One man pointedly asked McCain, "How did Barack Obama get where he is?" meaning in the polls, that is. McCain could not give a clear and truthful answer. But, we all know it was leadership that got Senator Barack Obama where he is today. Leadership my man! This is best stated by former President Bill Clinton, who, when asked to sum up the Obama factor simply replied, Senator Barack Obama has the "best ability and best supporting cast." ("Barack Obama: Ready, Fit to Lead" New York *Daily Challenge* Newspaper, 2008, pp. 4-5).

BARACK OBAMA:
THE PEOPLE'S CHAMPION

BY DR. FRED MONDERSON

When a people have chosen their champion and send him forth to do battle, they're obligated to keep track of the unfolding of his fate. In fact, the people must track the progress, rise and fall and particularly pay attention to sidereal commentary, regarding his character, ideas, values, associations and demeanor, whether positive or negative. What is most important, however, the people's champion, having been charged, being knowledgeable about his mission and purpose, obviously recognizes the pitfalls; but understanding the significance of his mission, and what he represents to those under whose banner he fights, never lets such distractions dissuade him from his appointed tasks. What's obvious, first of all, Barack Obama, the people's champion, is African American. Perhaps Sir Walter Scott's (1771-1832) description of the likes of Senator Barack Obama in *Marmion* is apropos here, in his offering when he speaks of: "His square-turn's joints, and strength of limbs, showed him no carpe knight so trim, But in close fight a champion grim, in camps a leader sage."

As so many have accepted this and sent him forth under their banner, they must consistently pay attention to those planting the minefield along the path their champion must traverse. As such, then, the anti-personnel barbs strewn in Senator Barack Obama's path to the White

House, range from attempts to link him with Osama Bin Laden, to being a black man. The latter we know, all the others are spurious.

Looking at this phenomenon, Barack Obama, the first black man chosen to represent a major political party in America, has been accused of not being black enough, then being too black. Then he was accused of being too liberal, a Muslim, a "Wrightist," unpatriotic and not-wearing the American flag pin on his lapel. As if that's not enough, he was accused of being anti-American, "palling around with terrorists," and while he first voted in the senate against the war in Iraq, he was then accused of wanting to lose that same war in Iraq. Barack Obama was accused of not remembering the name of an Iraq soldier whose bracelet he was wearing on his wrist.

Along the way, the Republican challenger's camp sought to acquire Barack Obama's birth certificate to use whatever personal information to their advantage. As some have said, "everyday there is a new attack on Obama." He was also accused of being a Marxist, socialist, implying communist tendencies. Late in the campaign, Senator Obama was accused of being a "distributor" for wanting to "distribute the wealth" as he told "Joe the Plumber" regarding the strategy of his tax plan. He and his wife Michelle were parodied as Arabs on the cover of the New Yorker magazine and Senator McCain had to correct a woman at one of his campaign stops, that Senator Obama is "not an Arab. He is a citizen, a decent man with a family and we have disagreements over positions."

I guess, to these, as in *Paradise Regained* John Milton (1608-1674) would say: "Calling shapes and beckoning shadows dire, and airy tongues that syllable men's names, On sands, and shores, and desert wilderness. These thoughts may startle well, but not astound, the virtuous mind, that ever walks attended, by a strong siding champion, Conscience."

And even further, "The childhood shows the man, as morning shows the day. Be famous then by wisdom; as thy empire must extend, so let extend thy mind o'er the world."

Last but not least, the McCain/Palin team has harped on a six-month old Los Angeles *Times* article about a 2003 meeting at which Obama attended and a Palestinian activist was also there. The L.A. *Times* refused to release a tape of the gathering on the principle of non-disclosure to its original owner. When the McCain camp was asked why bring up this six month old article, their only response was "Because Senator Obama is one week away from being President."

Interesting, when former Secretary of State Colin Powell, a Republican, endorsed Senator Barack Obama, a Democrat, he described him as being a "transformational figure," who will bring about "generational change." Regarding Senator Obama being associated with terrorists among the many attacks leveled against him, Secretary Powell thought such charges "a terrible stretch of demagoguery." Conversely, the Anchorage *Daily News* in Alaska, Governor Sarah Palin's hometown newspaper, in endorsing Senator Obama, said he "brings far more promise to the office. In a time of grave economic crisis, he displays thoughtful analysis, enlists wise counsel and operates with a cool, steady hand." In addition, newspaper said, Senator Obama had "judgment and intelligence to shape a solution, as well as the leadership to rally the country behind it."

When we contemplate the many attack accusations leveled on the integrity of Barack Obama by the Republican Party and his opponents Senator John McCain and his running mate, Sarah Palin, these accusations have colored the complexity of this race to be President of the United States.

However, in a note on reality, an analogy is a useful tool that lets us make causal connections between ideas and experiences. Everyone is familiar with the Biblical story of Noah and the flood when he made his selections for the voyage of the ark. Now, in America, while there's no Noah as Captain, we could, however, conjure up a case similar in substance to Noah's action. As Obama chooses the occupants of America's ark, he is sure to include Christians, Jews, Catholics, Muslims, agnostics, atheists, gays, lesbians, handicaps, criminals, mafia, etc. However, just before the captain would close the hatch, someone would probably shout, "Don't leave those two racists, and the two Klansmen next to them, for they are part of America's past, present and future."

Now, when Governor Sarah Palin, in her incendiary rancor stoked the fire of elements eager to exhibit their racist underbelly, what these simpleminded miscreants were incapable of recognizing, these times are different to African Americans' ancestors' times. The African, enslaved, freed, exposed to unspeakable horrors during and after slavery; endured to persevere to provide the wherewithal for progeny. What these descendants have proved, they too love this country and will not countenance others "putting sand in their rice."

Even the latest flap uttered by Senator Biden, Obama's running mate, that: "It will not be six months before the world tests Barack Obama like it did John Kennedy," elicited a response from John McCain who said: "We don't want a president who invites testing from the world at a time when our economy is in crisis and Americans are already fighting in two wars." Metaphorically speaking, having waged a vicious and unrelentingly negative campaign, McCain's side finally threw the kitchen sink at which Obama side-stepped and it missed. Then McCain rolled out "Joe the Plumber," and announced at Al Smith's Dinner "I have fired my entire staff and replaced them with 'Joe the Plumber.'" This "instant celebrity" soon began doing the media rounds, stumps with Sarah Palin, and prognosticated about Obama's position on Israel on McCain's behalf! Imagine! To speak about foreign policy, what are Joe's qualifications!! Additionally, it turns out Joe is not even a licensed plumber, which means McCain will hire 'Unprofessional" help. More important, however, while Senator McCain hoped to make hay of Senator Obama, that as President he would be tested, is another symptom the Senator's inadequate assessment of the state of things. That line of argument presupposes the world will not test McCain as President. Does Senator McCain, admitting we're at war on two fronts, challenged by Al Qaeda and all the other bad boys, who will "stand down" because McCain is President? Will these same troublemakers not test Sarah Palin, if she were to succeed John McCain?

The problem with Sarah Palin's analysis of Senator Biden's statement is not only to show how shallow her thinking is, but also to depict her one-sidedness. We have credited Senator Biden with being a foreign policy expert with tons of years in the Senate. In this, experience has taught him America's enemies will challenge the next president, whoever he or she is. We talk about two wars in Iraq and Afghanistan as well as the threats from "rogue states," but maliciously presume they won't pose a threat if John McCain is president. Therefore, if Governor Palin succeeds President McCain these same enemies will challenge her, being a woman and inexperienced as well. Much more important is how the people's champion, Barack Obama, has been challenged, maligned, as attempts were made to sidetrack his campaign from the time of the Democratic Primary and then through the contest between the Republican and Democratic Presidential Candidates. ("Barack Obama: The People's Champion" *Daily Challenge* Newspaper, November 3, 2008, pp. 4-5)

THE BLACK MAN: "DID IT."

BY DR. FRED MONDERSON

While Voltaire said, "Crush the Accursed thing," regarding Friday the 13th, such an admonition ought to be applied to the notion of the "Bradley Effect;" because Barack Obama has worked tremendously and untiring, in a unifying campaign with a powerful message, to make this an issue of the past! His aura and its attraction of diverse people, as evident from his recent rallies makes one feel confident "Bradley," is no more. What has been bothersome, however, is people like the "blond-headed woman," hopefully in the minority, at one of Senator McCain's rallies who described Senator Barack Obama as "an unaccomplished black man," who aspires to be President of the United States of America. Clearly such an ignoramus would not know an accomplished "black man," if, as E.F. Hutton's spokesman used to say, "He showed up, slap you on the bottom, and said I'm here." Even more important, across this great nation, untold numbers of intellectual "black men" are doing wonderful things to assist the Barack Obama presidential campaign, despite the fact, much of this is not known; which could also be a good thing! That poor, misguided soul would weep, if she really knew how empty her assertion really is!

Barack Obama is a Columbia University graduate; a Harvard University law graduate; and he was President of the Harvard University Law Review. Everyone knows he was a Community Organizer in Chicago.

Subsequently he became an Illinois State Senator and later became a Federal Senator from Illinois. He authored two books! As the son of a single mother who died early, whose father abandoned him, he was raised by his grandmother, and where he is today is clearly a significant accomplishment! For Obama to be competing with John McCain for the Presidency, against a man born with "a gold spoon" in his mouth, Obama's "silver spoon" sure looks polished today! His eloquence, intellectual fortitude, cool demeanor, social adjustment and attractiveness outdistances his opponent, the "Admiral's son." And Senator McCain is wrong, Senator Obama is not just measuring the drapes, he's picking a cabinet, checking the guest list and planning the celebration party! Unfortunately such individuals as the "blond lady," thank God they're in the minority, could never understand, the accomplished "black man" is often times more accomplished than his white counterpart. For as the saying goes, "the black man cannot be on the same level as his white counterpart to get the job, he has to be better." Nevertheless, it may be helpful to historically sketch an example of the path the black man has had to travel in this country on the road to becoming accomplished! And, considering the organization of Senator Obama's presidential campaign is reflective of his success in this respect; one can say gained from his experience of being in the trenches as a Community Organizer.

Some commentators believe the "black man" is an endangered species, but an even more daunting specter surrounds the "black man," for whether he is Senator Barack Obama or the man in the street, it can equally apply. Interesting, if a United States Senator, a distinguished individual, could be subject to invidious name calling, threats, innuendos, false accusations, etc., imagine what type of victimization the average "black man" is susceptible to. Nevertheless, lest we forget, Philip Forde, a "black man" stands atop the Capital dome in D.C. Therefore, to understand this phenomenal predicament across the American historical and political landscape, one has to look at the history of how Americans have treated the "black man" for much of his time in this country. However, today, the world is now looking on as this election unfolds, and it's even more important the wrong impression is not conveyed through the actions of many who exhibit racist behaviors. This notwithstanding, it's important that we sketch the "evolution of the black man" to civil tendencies and financial and social accomplishment, despite the many hurdles he has to scale on his way to the top!

First of all, as Malcolm X has pointed out, all peoples who came to America, viz., Chinese, Japanese, Indian, Italian, German, Swede, Englishman, Irish, etc., upon their arrival here remained Chinese, Japanese, Indian, Italian, German, Swede, Englishman, Irish, etc. All, except the African who was kidnapped, brought across the Atlantic Ocean, chained in the most dreadful manner, subjected to unspeakable trans-Atlantic horrors, denied his manhood, dehumanized and disrespected over the centuries of slavery, until he was finally freed by Abraham Lincoln. This magnanimous act became legal under the Civil War Amendments, wherein the thirteenth legalized his freedom, the fourteenth make him a citizen and the fifteenth gave him the right to vote. Thereafter, the freedman struggled to regain his manhood, acquire a sense of human decency, and reflect and demonstrate social civility and citizenship within the strictures accorded him in the society he helped to build, generation after generation, laboring for free.

As all of this transpired, as Kenneth Stampp has written about slavery, in *The Peculiar Institution*, a chapter entitled: "To Make Them Stand in Fear;" while amazingly, the freedman metamorphosed through being an African, then slave, freedman, ex-slave, Negro, colored, black and today African American, with a whole host of disgusting epithets also applied to him, along the way, in the most demeaning manner. Complementing this state of affairs, the "black man" remained black in the minds and actions of many persons who sought to demean and accuse him, to cover their misgivings, or to further their own aims. At the end of all this, he was asked to forgive his slave master and his descendants, and to overlook the wealth they accumulated as they perpetrated, at his expense, unspeakable horrors through the duration of the slavery experience, and then deny his 40 acres and a mule.

While Chief Justice Taney's *Dred Scott* Decision of 1857 and *Plessy v. Ferguson* of 1896, generally defined the status and position of the "black man," during the period of Reconstruction and in the age of Jim Crow, terror groups as the Ku Klux Klan (KKK), Knights of the White Camellia, as well as several stratagems were employed to terrorize, intimidate and keep the "black man" "in his place." In the South, to keep the "black man" from expressing his right to vote under the Fifteenth Amendment, literacy tests, poll tax, property tax, grandfather clause and particularly election site shenanigans were effectively employed to nullify the "black man's" vote. Whippings, tar and feather, killings, lynchings, burnings, destruction of house and homes, and all forms of odious behaviors were resorted to in order to halt the "back man's" forward progress in those dark days of the "Birth of the Nation."

While only a dozen cases need suffice, Ralph Ginsburg's *100 Years of Lynching*, Baltimore, MD., Black Classics Press (1962) 1988, chronicles untold numbers of the most hideous forms of "white behavior" towards the "black man." Most, particularly those chosen were committed against innocent "black men,' and importantly it shows the uncontrollable rage of the mob fueled by the belief in white supremacy.

1. "**New York Truth Seeker.** April 17, 1880. "First Negro at West Point Knifed by Fellow Cadets." West Point, N.Y. Apr. 15. – James Webster Smith, the first colored cadet in the history of West Point, was recently taken from his bed, gagged, bound, and severely beaten, and then his ears were slit. He says that he cannot identify his assailants. The other cadets claim that he did it himself." (p. 9) This is difficult to understand how he could raise himself from his bed, gag and bound himself, then severely whip himself and finally cut his own ear. One has to wonder, who was the Commanding Officer who believed this story?

2. "**Chicago Tribune**. November 22, 1895. "Texans Lynch Wrong Negro." Madisonville, Tex, Nov. 21 – News has been received here of the lynching of a Negro in this part of Madison County on Tuesday night. He was accused of riding his horse over a little white girl and injuring her. On Wednesday it was discovered that the wrong Negro had been gotten hold of by the mob. The guilty one made his escape." (p. 21) Question is, how many Negroes had horses to ride around, that such a mistake could be made.

3. "**New York Times.** June 11, 1900. "An Innocent Man Lynched." New Orleans, June 10 – A mob willfully and knowingly

handled and burned an innocent man, as well as another who was probably innocent, near Mississippi City, Miss., between midnight and 1 o'clock this morning. The lynching was the result of impatience on the part of the people of Biloxi, a nearby town, over the failure of the officers of the law to produce the man who a week ago murdered Christina Winterstein, a schoolgirl who was returning to her home near Biloxi after attending the commencement exercises at her school." (p. 31) So they go about grabbing whoever they find. The gall of these people

4. "**Houston Post.** June 11, 1900. "Two Blacks Strung Up; Grave Doubt of Their Guilt." Biloxi, Miss., June 10 – Lynch law ran rampant in this section last night. Two Negro men were lynched, possibly for one man's crime, early this morning at Mississippi City, and it is not absolutely certain that either victim of mob law was guilty. Henry Askew and Ed Russ, held as suspects, were taken out and strung up to a tree in a thicket, just behind the railway station at Mississippi City." (p. 32) Where was the Governor, Mayor, Police Commissioner, Sheriff or Marshal when the mob ruled?

5. **Chicago Record-Herald** may 12, 1901. "Believes Wrong Man Lynched." Birmingham, Ala., May 11 – A Negro supposed to be James Brown, accused of assaulting Miss Della Garrett of Springsville, was shot and killed by a number of white men near Leeds, near here, to-day. The coroner is of the opinion that the wrong man has been killed." (p. 39) Who investigated this incident and what action was taken? For an assault, you kill a man as if his life had no value.

6. **Chicago Record-Herald**, July 27, 1903. "Wrong Man Lynched as Rapist." Savannah, Ga., July 26 – Several days ago a Negro supposed to be Ed Claus, was lynched near Eastman, Ga., for assaulting Miss Susie Johnson, a young school teacher. The Negro protested he was not Claus and asked for time to prove his statement. But the mob was merciless. It now transpires that the Negro was not Claus and had never seen Miss Johnson. Claus, who assaulted the girl, has been located near Narien, Ga., and officers passed through here tonight to secure him. It is believed Claus will be taken from the officers and lynched." (p. 60) They never gave him a chance to present

his ID. One has to wonder what these people felt and did when it was realized they had killed an innocent man. Not satisfied with one life for an assault, they took another!

7. **New York Press.** March 26, 1904. "9 Lynchings in One Week." Little Rock, Ark., March 25 – A special from Dewitt says five Negroes have been taken from the guards at St. Charles, this county, and shot to death by a mob. This makes nine negroes who have been killed in the last week in the vicinity of St. Charles on account of race troubles." (p. 69) What does history say of these men? The victims and those who perpetrated this heinous crime.

8. **Montgomery Advertiser**. September 12, 1912. "Lynched 'For Being Black.'" United States District Attorney O.D. Street, of Birmingham, today made public a letter which he is forwarding to Governor O'Neil. The letter is from C.P. Lunsford of Hackleburg, and reads as follows: "On last Wednesday there was a Negro man chased and hounded down and murdered while going peacefully along the railroad. There was not anything against him, but a party of men got after him because his skin was black and murdered him. The grand jury was in session at the time, and has not paid any attention to the murder, not even so much as to put the parties under arrest. The Negro who was murdered was Willie Perkins of Sheffield, and I am reliably informed that he was of an excellent character." (p. 77) So, "walking while black" is an old act of racial vindictiveness. One thing is certain; some men have no respect for the law!

9. **Harrisburg (Pennsylvania) Advocate Verdict**. September 13, 1912. "Wrong Man Believed Lynched." Princeton, W.VA., Sept. 7 – That a mistake was made in lynching Walter Johnson, a colored man last night, is now believed by the authorities. A statement was issued by Mayor Bennington, Sheriff Ellison, Judge Maynard and Prosecuting Attorney J.O. Pendleton stating that there is plenty of evidence that Walter Johnson did not commit the crime for which he was lynched. A mob lynched Johnson last night, allegedly for attacking Nite White, 14-year old daughter of a railroad man. Today's statement said that Johnson fell far short in dress and physical appearance of the man described by the girl." (p. 78) Question is, what did these public officials do to and for the victim's family?

10. **Chicago Tribune**. December 31, 1914. "1914 Lynchings Show Rise." The number of lynchings in 1914 shows a small increase over that of 1913, being 54, as compared with 48 in 1913 and 64 in 1912. The following table showing the annual number during the last thirty years may be of general interest.

1865	184	1900	115
1866	138	1901	130
1887	122	1902	96
1888	142	1903	104
1899	176	1904	87
1890	127	1905	60
1891	193	1906	60
1892	205	1907	65
1893	200	1908	100
1894	170	1909	87
1895	171	1910	74
1896	181	1911	71
1897	106	1912	64
1898	127	1913	48
1899	107	1914	54

(p. 94)

These numbers are mind-boggling and one has to wonder, How many were not recorded and also how many people were arrested, charged, convicted, and executed for their lawless terrorism.

11. **Atlanta Constitution**. February 23, 1916. "All Five Lynched Negroes Were Guiltless, Says Keith." Tefton, Ga., Feb. 22 – Jim Keith, sentenced to a life term in prison for complicity in the killing of Sheriff Moreland of Lee County, talked freely of the crime today as he was carried to Richmond County to begin serving his term. He declared that Rodius Seamore and old man Lake and his three sons, who were lynched last month

for Sheriff Moreland's death, were entirely guiltless. The fact is now generally believed." (pp. 99-100)

12. **New York Times**. May 27, 1961. "Attorney General Foresees a Negro as U.S. President." Washington, May 26 – Attorney General Robert F. Kennedy, in a broadcast to the world over the Voice of America, today acknowledged the United States' imperfections in the areas of equal rights for Negroes. He said, however, that progress was being made in that area so rapidly that "There's no question that in the next thirty or forty years a Negro can achieve the position ... of President of the United States. " (pp. 251-2520

We are all told Audie Murphy was the most decorated World War II veteran. Not so as Harry Belafonte told it. The most decorated World War II veteran was a "black man," who, returning to the South, in full uniform with his medals, rode in the front of a segregated bus. When the driver asked him to sit in the back, he refused. The driver called the police to remove the "black man" in uniform. The brutes killed him on the spot. Harry says this is what led him to become an activist. In more modern times, Massachusetts Governor Michael Dukakis was the 1988 Democratic standard-bearer and in that election for President, the Republicans waded into him, using the sinister "black man" smear and fear tactic. Apparently, as Governor, Dukakis issued some form of release to a convict named Willie Horton, who, upon gaining his freedom, attacked and killed a woman. The Republican candidate, the first George Bush, pounced on this and made a fuss about the weakness or softness of Dukakis on crime, while playing up the notion of the sinister "black man." Naturally, Dukakis lost the election as his opponents proclaimed the brilliance of their strategy. In fact, what they had done is, reinforce the specter that the "black man" is bad and this rationalizes the attacks, charges, claims, insinuations, etc. that generates fear in the minds of whites. This fear is probably even more widespread, as it even allows law enforcement officers to stop the "black man," in "stop and frisk" and most often "driving while black!"

Not so long ago, the "Smith woman," involved in a love affair of some sort, rolled her car with two children in the back seat, into a pond. Then she confused the investigation by claiming a "black man" attacked her, high-jacked her car, and kidnapped her two children. In time, the lie was bared, and as she broke down, she confessed her story was a hoax; and then showed where she had disposed of the car and kids. She was considered mentally disturbed and that was that.

In Jasper, Texas, within recent memory, a "black man," I think, Brandon McClelland, who was chained to a pick-up truck and dragged to his death. The more things change, the more they remain the same.

A man in Massachusetts killed his wife and children then claimed a "black man" invaded their home and did the beastly act. This gristly crime helped fan the hysteria against the "black man." Naturally he confessed to the wrongdoing, for which he had blamed the "black man." Only recently, Ashley claimed a "black man" robbed her at an ATM, and noticing she had a McCain/Palin sticker on her bumper, carved a "B" on her cheek. The bank's cameras did not even pick up her presence there nor did it record any assault nearby. Turns out the story was false, but the nut was later admitted to a program.

The above are only a sample of instances where the "black man" was innocently harassed, victimized, killed and falsely accused, and all because of his race. Notwithstanding, sometimes symbolism means more than substance, and for the descendants of those who traversed the incendiary strewn, social minefield, of American society, the Obama candidacy, while substantive, is also more symbolic for the millions of African Americans in this country, and so many "black men" worldwide. The significance of the Obama candidacy is, internally it demonstrates a coming of age of America particularly in view of its emerging multi-ethnicity; and externally to the world it signaled a radical change in America's personality and image, for which its true nature as the world leader will manifest.

Well Mr. Kennedy, having said all of that, it actually took 47 years in a long and arduous walk to the White House. But, most important, "the Black man" did it, despite the distractions, odds, and it shows while this significant milestone has been reached, there is still more work to be done to achieve Dr. King's color-blind society, that judges a person based on intellect and integrity rather than rage and race. ("The Black Man Did it!" New York *Daily Challenge* Newspaper, November 6, 10-11, pp. 4-5.2008)

"The man for the Moment."
By Hillary Clinton. New York *Daily News*,
Sunday, November 2, 2008.

Former Democratic Presidential Candidate Hillary Rodham Clinton penned an exclusive *Daily News* op-ed piece, in which she exhorted New Yorkers to vote for Barack Obama as president, because "he'll take America forward." When one thinks about the strange competitiveness of the Primary, then the power of forgiveness, "kiss and make up," is great when the sake of a party triumph means so much. Mrs. Clinton campaigned unrelentingly for Senator Obama; so much so, many people want to credit his victory in Florida as a Clinton gift. Nevertheless, in her piece, Hillary asks the question about the alternative to Obama? Then she explained: "We find ourselves in an economic crisis born and bred by the failed policies of Washington Republicans: cut regulations; cut taxes for billionaires and big corporations instead of the middle class; continue tax breaks for oil companies, drug companies, insurance companies, and companies that ship jobs overseas; deny the home mortgage crisis; ignore the energy crisis; and dismiss the health care crisis."

Then she gives some results of those policies on American society, where: "Businesses can't find credit. Students can't find college loans. Retirees' nest eggs are starting to crack. I've met hardworking men and women near retirement who are afraid to check their 401 (k)s. Health care premiums have doubled. On Thursday, we learned that the economy actually contracted in the last three months. And the United States has lost jobs for nine straight months; President Bush has the worst job creation record of any President since the Great Depression...."

Even further, she offered: "The Republicans' answer to jobs being outsourced: continue tax incentives to companies that outsource jobs. Their answer to a broken health care system: throw everybody to the mercy of insurance companies. Their answer to rising economic insecurity: privatize Social Security. Their answer to rising costs and stagnant wages: trickle down tax cuts for millionaires instead of middle class families."

Then she states Senator Obama's position as outlined in his many campaign speeches. She wrote: "Obama has proposed a tax cut for 95% of people earning a paycheck. He'll fight for equal pay for equal work. He'll protect Social Security. And Obama will promote policies that reflect the way parents are working and living today, including child care, long term care, and a stronger Family and Medical Leave Act. Obama will invest new jobs in clean energy, manufacturing and infrastructure. And he'll fight for universal health care."

"Obama's Heroic Achievement."
By Rev. Al Sharpton in New York's *Daily News*, Wednesday, November 5, 2008, p. 23.

The Reverend Al Sharpton, President of National Action Network clarified the meaning of Obama's win in the national elections in the statement: "…the country as a whole should be proud because Obama's candidacy was never truly hobbled or engulfed by the issue of race. Instead, the American people adhered to the Rev. Martin Luther King's standard that a man be judged by the content of his character rather than the color of his skin."

Arguing that the Obama Presidency does not represent a "post civil right era," Rev. Sharpton opined: "Such arguments misread the tea leaves swirling through America. The fact remains that, although the nation is willing to make important and laudatory exceptions to the "race rule," it still exists. African-Americans are not treated equally as a people and must struggle for equality every day. This doesn't change after Obama's remarkable run."

"…the issues that stoke the smoldering embers beneath the discussion of race and racism are still with us even while Obama soars. Just last year, hangman nooses dotted the countryside of the very states that Obama campaigned in so effectively. The tragedy of Sean Bell, the innocent man gunned down by police, happened during this election season. The Jenna 6 case (in which black teenagers were treated much more harshly than their white counterparts despite causing similar mischief) and the Genarlow Wilson case (in which a teenager got a prison sentence for having oral sex with a fellow teenager) are both signs of an unequal justice system slow to change."

"Leaders like me must keep Obama accountable…"

"We should always understand that whoever our first black President would be, he would be leader of all the people, not just black America. Further, we must recognize that without the appropriate consciousness-raising by civil rights leaders, race issue could either doom such a leader to a failed one-term presidency or doom America to remaining hostage to its inglorious racial past."

"…there is still much work for me and other civil rights leaders to do."

"We Rise and Fall as One Nation" is what some have entitled Barack Obama's acceptance speech in Chicago. Here, President-Elect Barack Obama poured out his heart and honesty, demonstrated that intellectual prowess in grasp of ideas and superb oratory, as he explained to the American people the significance of his success and the challenges that lay ahead and how they can all work together for the betterment of America. In this he said:

"If there is anyone out there who still doubts that America is a place where all things are possible; who still wonders if the dream of our founders is alive in our time; who still questions the power of our democracy, tonight is your answer."

"It's the answer spoken by young and old, rich and poor, Democrat and Republican, black, white, Latino, Asian, Native American, gay, straight, disabled and not disabled - Americans who sent a message to the world that we have never been a collection of Red States and Blue States: We are, and always will be, the United States of America."

"…change has come to America."

The greatest challenges lay ahead with two wars in Iraq and Afghanistan, but he praised the American fighting man over there, doing his duty.

"The road ahead will be long. Our climb will be steep. We may not get there in one year or even one term, but America - I have never been more hopeful than I am tonight that we will get there. I promise you - we as a people will get there. ... I will ask you join in the work of remaking this nation the only way it's been done in America for 221 years - block by block, brick by brick, calloused hand by calloused hand."

Then he speaks of patriotism, service, responsibility and hard work.

"Let us remember that if this financial crisis taught us anything, it's that we cannot have a thriving Wall Street while Main Street suffers - in this country, we rise or fall as one nation; as one people."

Quoting Abraham Lincoln, also from Illinois, he reflects, "We are not enemies, but friends ... though passion may have strained it must not break our bonds of affection. And to those Americans whose support I have yet to earn - I may not have won your vote, but I hear your voices, I need your help, and I will be your president too."

Then he addresses friends and foes abroad, saying, "And to all those watching tonight from beyond our shores, from parliaments and palaces to those who are huddled around radios in the forgotten corners of our world - our stories are singular, but our destiny is shared, and a new dawn of American leadership is at hand. To those who would tear this world down - we will defeat you. To those who seek peace and security - we support you. And to all those who have wondered if America's beacon still burns as bright - tonight we proved once more that the true strength of our nation comes not from the might of our arms or the scale of our wealth, but from the enduring power of our ideals: democracy, liberty, opportunity, and unyielding hope. For that is the true genius of America - that America can change. Our union can be perfected. And what we have already achieved gives us hope for what we can and must achieve tomorrow."

Obama was really impressed by the 106 year old Ann Nixon Cooper, of whom he says, "...a woman who cast her ballot in Atlanta. She's a lot like the millions of others who stood in line to make their voice heard in this election except for one thing: Ann Nixon Cooper is 106 years old. She was born just a generation past slavery; a time when there were no cars on the road or planes in the sky; when someone like her

65

couldn't vote for two reasons - because she was a woman and because of the color of her skin. And tonight, I think about all that she's seen throughout her century in America the heartache and the hope; the struggle and the progress; the times we were told that we can't, and the people who pressed on with that American creed: Yes we can."

"At a time when women's voices were silenced and their hopes dismissed, she lived to see them stand up and speak out and reach for the ballot. Yes we can. When there was despair in the dust bowl and depression across the land, she saw a nation conquer fear itself with a New Deal, new jobs and a new sense of common purpose. Yes we can. When the bombs fell on our harbor and tyranny threatened the world, she was there to witness a generation rise to greatness and a democracy was saved. Yes we can. She was there for the buses in Montgomery, the hoses in Birmingham, a bridge in Selma, and a preacher from Atlanta who told a people that "We Shall Overcome." Yes we can.

"A man touched down on the moon, a wall came down in Berlin, a world was connected by our own science and imagination. And this year, in this election, she touched her finger to a screen, and cast her vote, because after 106 years in America, through the best of times and the darkest of hours, she knows how America can change. Yes we can."

"This is our moment. This is our time to put our people back to work and open doors of opportunity for our kids; to restore prosperity and promote the cause of peace; to reclaim the American Dream and reaffirm that fundamental truth - that out of many, we are one; that while we breathe, we hope, and where we are met with cynicism, and doubt, and those who tell us that we can't, we will respond with that timeless creed that sums up the spirit of a people: Yes We Can."

"Thank you, God Bless you, and may God Bless the United States of America."

Well, I guess he said it all. Now the real part begins for while he has passed the theoretical test, the test of practicality now begins as Barack Obama, American citizen, President of the United States of America, President of all the people, is also a black man, an African American.

BARACK OBAMA: VICTORIOUS

BY DR. FRED MONDERSON

Barack Obama's recent big win in the presidential election was a victory for America, the Obama family, and even more than that, it was a victory for, as W.E.B. DuBois has said, "100 million African souls lost to Africa," many of whom were casualties of the Slave Trade and became victims of the Atlantic Ocean. Even more, the unknown and untold victims of the internal slave trade and institutional slavery; and the numerous blacks or African Americans who stood up to challenge America before and after it established the Declaration of Independence and the Constitution that crafted its credo of America as the "land of the free" and "home of the brave!" Whether it was Phyllis Wheatley, through her poetry, who stood up to convey the intellectual capabilities of the African in America; Denmark Vesey, Gabriel Prosser and Nat Turner who chose revolutionary means to challenge the system; Dred Scott; Martin Delaney, Frederick Douglass; Booker T. Washington; Marcus Garvey; Paul Robeson; Mary McLeod Bethune; A. Philip Randolph; Martin Luther King; Fannie Lou Hamer; Malcolm X; and so many others who paved the way. All this notwithstanding, Obama's victory had an even more significant meaning. Mr. Alvin Young believed, "It was providential, because nothing could have stopped this."

Perhaps there was some spiritual, mystical hand at work, maybe divine intervention, but it's reasonable to assume something bigger than all the combatants on the field, helped contribute to Senator Obama's victory. The weather was good and despite the numerous underhand and shady tactics designed to confuse and lead voters astray, none of that prevailed; and with reservoirs of patience, people were determined to register their approval of the winds of change sweeping the nation.

Accepting that a picture says a thousand words, the TV station CNN showed a picture of Senator Barack Obama, early in the day, leading his family into the polling place in Chicago, where he voted and the comment was made, "Here's a black man voting for himself for President of the United States." How profound! Of even greater significance, for more than two centuries of voting in America, in the ante-bellum south and north, and post-Civil War America, those blacks privileged to vote could only vote for a white candidate for the highest position in the land. Therefore, that image of Barack Obama carefully checking the list of candidates, taking his time to make sure he got it right, not wanting to hurriedly vote and end up giving McCain his vote; he reflected that air of confidence, self esteem, intellectual fortitude and the type of presidential timber that could have whispered to him, "Today you will make history, shake things up and outdistance the competition."

When we listen to the pundits, talking heads, spin meisters, their come around is one of extraordinary praise about the demeanor, fortitude, organizational ability, intellectual prowess and visionary capabilities of Barack Obama. This being so, one has to wonder about this new awakening the media is experiencing. If they had seen these traits in the man, they certainly did not show it, holding back until the election; and all of a sudden, an enormous burst of insightful and praiseworthy recognition that Barack Obama was a great man with enormous potential to change America. The confidence Senator Obama exuded, infected communities across the country and world; that is, from Harlem, the cultural capital of Black America to Holland in Europe, people confessed to being floored, undone, amazed, overwhelmed, and full of joy. Some believed such a triumph would never have occurred in their lifetime. For others, it was a bitter-sweet moment. Oprah Winfrey thought, "Anything is possible. It feels hope won." One Congressman said, "I will be able to tell my grandchildren, these hands that picked cotton, picked a President. They did not believe it could happen, neither did I." Some people directly suggested it was the hand of god at work. Congressman John Lewis thought it "An out of body experience" that Barack Obama could win so handily. All this could only happen in America. ("Barack Obama: Victorious" *Tactical Dojo News Magazine*, November 2008, p. 2)

CONVENTIONS, ELECTIONS AND OUR TIMES

BY DR. FRED MONDERSON

It began with Tiger Woods choosing not to play golf this year, and other players were in jubilation that some of them could win one title! Michael Phelps won a gold medal at the 2008 Olympics in China by $1/100^{th}$ of a second. Imagine! Sitting and looking at the clock strike a second and them divide that by 100. Talk about wasting time! Also, many people were asking whether "Fifty Cent" and "P-Diddy" are still relevant today. Nevertheless, this aside, there's much that has happened between the campaigns and the election, and bears some recapping. This can be divided into two parts. There are the things that happened to the candidate Senator Barack Obama and what had happened to the country he set out to be elected to rule. The latter can be synthesized in a statement written in an article entitled "The Mindset in the Middle," written by Peter Baker in the *New York Times*, November 2, 2008, Week in Review section, p. 3. He described the state of America today as: "Hundreds of thousands have lost their jobs. The national debt is skyrocketing. The Taliban rampaging through Afghanistan. Pakistan is a nuclear-armed shambles. The country is still at war in Iraq and trying to avoid it with Iran and North Korea. And much of the world hates us." Then he asks, why would anyone want the job to clean up this mess? Fortunately, the confidence Senator Barack Obama espoused signaled he wanted the job! More important, however, as an American and because he loves his country, Barack Obama wanted to rescue

America from its present quagmire and bring the necessary changes he envisioned.

In a national election with historical implications, the first black candidate of a major party, a woman to be Vice-President, all the stops were pulled out. The good, the bad, and sometimes the ugly practices were at work. Using dirty tricks in a presidential election seemed a Republican trademark, some say, reflecting all the goodies of the "Carl Rove Play Book." In retrospect, looking at the campaigns waged by both parties, clearly the Republicans were way more negative. One could suppose this is what turned voters off. Now let's look at some of what transpired.

First of all, Barack Obama was subjected to probably the most invidious attacks that essentially related to his race. He was accused of not being "black enough," then being "too black." Perhaps some of these accusers overlooked the fact he has a black wife, Michele and two black daughters, Malia and Sasha. They overlooked the fact he is a citizen and a distinguished person, being a United States Senator from the great state of Illinois. Still, the most interesting charge leveled at Barack was of being a Community Organizer, which was frowned upon by his political opponents. They seemed to say, grassroots work should not really count as experience. Little did Obama's opponents, particularly Sarah Palin, know, "you can learn a lot" from being a Community Organizer. Perhaps this mistake was their undoing for they certainly learned Senator Obama used this talent effectively.

As the Democratic Primary against Senator Hillary Rodham Clinton unfolded, and dragged out, the grass roots organization Obama created and nurtured, not only triumphed; but, by the time of the rigors of the Presidential race, particularly in the waning days, "his campaign experienced," as one pundit explained a "full body workout," and was thus able to meet the challenges down to the wire.

Barack Obama was accused of being inexperienced in foreign policy and leadership qualities. In response, he surrounded himself with the best American foreign policy, economic, energy and environmental minds, and in choosing Joe Biden as his running mate, added weight to his ticket. Next and consistently, Obama was accused of being a Muslim;

he was accused of "palling around with terrorists." While Ayers was a single "terrorist," the word "terrorists" seemed aimed at Muslims. Additionally, Senator Obama had to manage the Rev. Wright situation; Senator McCain kept asking "who is the real Barack Obama?" And finally "Joe the Plumber" coined the term "Socialism," and Senator McCain and Governor Sarah Palin began labeling Obama "Socialist." Yet still, Obama retained the high ground, not getting in the mud with his opponents and stayed on message with his ideas for tax relief for the middle class. Through it all, Obama debated, smiled, dug in, and rallied the troops while consistently envisioning the finish line. Did you see the *New York Post* political cartoon on Thursday, November 6, 2008, p. 24, showing Barack Obama saying "Bye-Bye Joe" as he flushed "Joe's Plumbing" down the bowl, with plunger and all!

When it comes to dirty tricks designed to mislead voters, the south was particularly funky. In West Virginia, for example, flyers and phone calls went out primarily to Democratic voters, Blacks, telling them Republicans vote on November 4th and Democrats on November 5th. Word circulated that Spanish voting is November 9th. Some people were told the election was postponed until next Wednesday. Some people were purged from election rolls without any good reason. CNN received some 60,000 phone calls about voting irregularities. There were mechanical problems, long lines, missing voter rolls, some coercion and intimidation. Even the problem of rain-soaked ballots had to be resolved. Nevertheless, these efforts proved futile. In addition, there were other entities doing the same call-in service, and lawyers across the country were mobilized to help in any way. Everybody was working to keep this election honest.

Secondly, many persons with insights made remarkable and incisive comments about their impressions, thoughts, and feelings about the results. For example, in recounting the names of many martyrs of the Civil Rights Movement, Jessie Jackson said he was overwhelmed with joy and pain, while John Lewis termed Barack Obama's victory a "non-violent revolution." Even Pat Robertson, the former Republican Presidential candidate was impressed saying, Obama ran an amazing campaign and he "could be one of the great presidents." He further thought Obama a "combination of the Messiah and Moses!" Martin

Luther King III thought the campaign and win "incredibly wonderful." Saying this was a major milestone, he believed his "mom and dad were smiling down on America." Mr. King made known, President-Elect "Obama possesses incredible vision; he is incredibly bright; and has the potential to become one of the greatest presidents of the United States of America."

One elderly woman termed the whole event "marvelous," and on Radio station Kiss FM 98.7, New York, a Social Studies 6th Grade teacher in Paling County, wherever that is, complained the district leaders did not want them to teach about the election. Imagine. Such a position seems bent on denying minority children a fundamental understanding of the workings of American government which shapes its history. Even more significant, however, this is an attempt to deny those children knowledge of their cultural history. Such a mindset is in keeping with ante-bellum mentality to keep blacks ignorant of their past, so they not know of the untold sufferings of their ancestors. As it's been said, "ignorance is bliss." Therefore, we must make sure the youth know of the trials, tribulations and triumphs of the African American experience. It is like my friend Wilbour Johnson said in his assessment of this phenomenal outcome. "'Yes we can' is a good slogan. 'Yes we did' is a testimony to what we can achieve as American citizens working together. That is, despite the struggles of the Civil Rights era. However, as we celebrate the victory of Barack Obama, we must consider grooming the young people to equal Obama's achievement." He continued further, "We must re-adjust young folks' vision of the future in light of this significant achievement, so that there are many more Barack Obamas. We must work to make sure this magnanimous election result is not a fluke and that, just as the elder Civil Rights activists passed the baton to the likes of Barack Obama, so too must our young be ready to receive it when he passes it to them."

In this day and age, such actions as in Paling County convey racial overtones. This seems contradictory to an accepted belief that race didn't seem a significant factor in the election. That is, despite the McCain/Palin team injecting "Who is the real Barack Obama?" and "he doesn't see America like we do." While they tried to play the Rev. Wright card, Barack trumped them, so this ploy was ineffective. When they played the Richard Ayres card by accusing Obama of "palling around with terrorists," most people didn't but it. When Colin Powell, a Republican, endorsed Barack Obama, a Democrat, he described the Ayers charge as "a stretch toward demagoguery."

In post-election commentary, TV reports described pandemonium at Ebenezer Baptist Church in Atlanta, where Dr. King preached. From this historic house of prayer, nursery of the Civil Rights Movement, the success of Barack Obama represented, as Oprah Winfrey believed, "a shift in consciousness because something big and bold happened in America." Equally too, Jesse Jackson, a familiar at Ebenezer, was caught on tape crying among the hundreds of thousands who gathered in the Park to hear Senator Obama either acknowledge or concede the results. When asked on TV to explain his tears, Jesse explained he felt a sense of joy in the tears, and remembering the long and difficult journey he described America as "a work in progress." Saying he voted six times for Barack Obama, twice as a State Senator, twice as Federal Senator and twice for the President; then he assessed Barack Obama as: "The best our struggle has to offer. The best America has to offer. This makes the tent even bigger. We must remember to praise the people who laid the foundation, Rosa Parks, Fannie Lou Hamer, Martin Luther King, and the many others." Teddy Cubia of Brooklyn said: "When I first heard Obama speak, I said this is the one to represent us. At the start of the year, I didn't know of him, now the world knows who Barack Obama is."

Even more, while a Harlemite thought Obama's triumph the "fulfillment of Martin Luther King's dream," former Secretary of State Colin Powell described the Obama campaign as being "all inclusive for it reached out across racial and religious lines. Barack Obama is a new President who also happens to be African American."

These are some of the issues that have engaged Americans and the world lately. This and much more will be issues of discussion for decades to come. ("Conventions, Elections and Our Times" New York *Daily Challenge* Newspaper 20, 2008, pp. 4-5).

Barack Obama: The Nuts and Bolts

By Dr. Fred Monderson

Who would ever believe a community Organizer could run such a near flawless national campaign that would end with a 7 million data base of supporters who could respond to the candidate's call to action.

All of this notwithstanding, there must have been a spiritual, metaphysical force at work that added the extra resolve to the efforts of all contributing to the resounding victory.

Looking back at Governor Palin scoffing at Barack Obama as a Community Organizer, in the aftermath of the election and deconstructing her stances, we become more aware of how shallow her analyses and posturing were.

"Today is the day that Americans make history" was the buzz on local radio, and after an earth-shattering day of near record voting, at the end of the day, Barack Obama confessed, "Tonight change has come to America."

One very elderly woman described the day as "marvelous" and admitted, "God kept me here for a purpose." Monique McDowell, 26-years old, from Denver, Colorado, said the election was "not about race, it's about issues in my state," and elsewhere across the country. Another, discussing racial change and generational change, proudly demonstrated joy and enthusiasm, and explained "for years African Americans were told what they can't do, not it's what we are and what can be."

Roger Clegg, President and General Counsel for the Center for Equal Opportunity in "The Prez-Elect's Quota Challenge" published in the *New York Post*, November 7, 2008, p. 33, discussed, on the one hand, his "mixed feelings" regarding President-Elect Barack Obama's position on race. Whereas: "On the other hand, Barack Obama is very liberal, so of course his administration is likely to be very liberal, too. Christopher Edley, an aggressive proponent of racial preferences, is a part of Obama's transition team. And it is very hard to persuade the left that racial preferences are a bad idea. On the other hand, Obama is not stupid, and especially not when it comes to law, policy and politics. He knows that the legal arguments for racial discrimination are shrinking." Still, as the old adage holds, "One sparrow does not make summer." This country was founded amidst discrimination and racial prejudice during the institution of slavery. The Three Fifths Clause, Northwest Ordinance, Abolitionism, Dred Scott, a Civil War, the 13th, 14th, and 15th Amendments, Reconstruction, Jim Crow, lynchings in the nadir, Plessy v. Ferguson, Grand-father Clause, Brown v. Board of Education of Topeka, Kansas, President Johnson's Great Society, with its Civil Rights and Voting Rights legislation, racial dragging, and Jim Crow, Jr. Esq., in his business suit. These things don't go away easily. Therefore, President-Elect Obama has to do a lot of wiggling in his little room, but confidence dictates he will address racial disparities in his own way.

However, continued Clegg, "If Obama is serious about being a unifying president – who reaches across the aisle, who isn't beholden to narrow and special party interest and, more fundamentally, who demands that Americans be treated without regard to race – he will end racial preferences."

Notwithstanding as the song says, "I might fly away, but not today."

Another way of looking at these issues can be gleaned from Melanie L. Campbell's "Vote for Obama on Nov. 4th: Voters, Know Your Rights Before You Go" in *Afro Times* November 1, 2008, Cover, points to tricks targeting the vote of African Americans who may potentially vote for Barack Obama on Election day. In this she asks: "Who are the enemies of voters? The enemy of voters are those politicians, elitists and advocates who spend countless hours creating policies and economic advantage over the masses – from unjust state voter ID laws to Black households receiving anonymous mailings with false information about what day they need to vote or being told if they have a traffic ticket or if their home has been foreclosed on, they will be arrested if they show up to vote. Isn't this contemporary racism?"

Even more important, Miriam Wright Edelman's "In this Election the Supreme Court Matters" in *Afro Times* November 1, 2008, p. 4, comments on the likelihood Barack Obama, as Chief Executive may have the power to appoint two or three judges to the supreme Court. Then she explained: "Federal judges are appointed to life terms and preside over cases involving a broad range of issues affecting children and working families including health care, education, civil rights and child safety. For example, in June 2008, the Supreme Court struck down Washington, D.C.'s ban on handguns in its ruling in the *District of Columbia v. Heller* case. This decision puts at risk numerous state and local statues and ordinances designed to remove guns from our streets at a time when gun deaths among children are on the rise." Her prescription is that, "For justice to be served, the next President must select nominees for federal courts with an eye toward advancing a positive vision of the law through a living Constitution that champions fairness, justice and equality for all." ("Barack Obama: The Nuts and Bolts" New York *Daily Challenge* Newspaper, 2008, pp. 4-5)

BARACK OBAMA: CONCLUSIONS

First let us congratulate President-Elect Barack Obama on his historic and magnanimous win in the recently concluded national elections. Let us be honestly euphoric about the significance of this historic moment, recognizing that African Americans have come a long was through the dark and stormy night of slavery, racial discrimination, racist violence and the most unimaginable horrors. Let us recognize a new day has dawned where a great many Americans put faith in a black man to lead this country. He needs the support of all well-meaning people, and we should give it to him unquestionably. However, let us never forget the nature of divine providence and the hand of God at work. Reverend Herbert Daughtry, "The People's Preacher," wrote an interesting piece in the *Daily Challenge*, November 7-9, 2008, entitled "Obama – Thank god." He wrote: "I started this article with a prayer of Thanksgiving. I saw the finger prints of God all over Obama and his campaign. In an article I wrote in this paper on February 28, 2008, I raised the question, that there was something uncanny, strange, and mysterious about Obama and his campaign. I tried hard not to invoke the name of God. I'm always reluctant to interpret human events with reference to God. However, there was no rational explanation for Obama's success. I'm even more convinced now that there was divine intervention. Even Obama, in his victory speech said, 'I was never the likeliest candidate for this office. We didn't start with much money or many endorsements.

Our campaign was not hatched in the halls of Washington. It began in the backyards of Des Moines and the living rooms of Concord and the front porches of Charleston.' The Bible teaches that God chooses the weak, the foolish, the things that the world rejects to effectuate his purpose that no flesh should glory in His presence."

Rev. Daughtry also invoked the names of the "martyrs" of black struggle whom he described as "ecstatic. Somewhere up there or out there." "The framers of the Amendments to the Constitution must be ecstatic!! The 13th amendment abolished slavery. The 14th conferred citizenship. And, the 15th gave the right to vote. Fred Douglas, Harriet Tubman, Sojourner Truth, Rev. Henry Highland Garnet, Bishop McNeil Turner, Ida B. Wells, A. Philip Randolph, and the Pullman Porters, Medgar Evers, Roy Wilkins and the National Association for Advancement of Colored People (NAACP), James Farmer, Floyd McKissick and the Congress of Racial Equality (CORE), Walter White, Whitney Young, and the Urban League, Kwame Toure, James foreman and Student Nonviolent Coordinating Committee (SNCC), Fannie Lou Hamer, Aaron Henry and the Mississippi Freedom Democratic Party, Bob Moses and the students of the Mississippi Summer Project, Michael Schwerner, Andrew Goodman, James Chaney, Ella Baker, Malcolm X, Dr. Martin Luther King Jr. and the Southern Christian Leadership Conference (SCLC), all who gave their lives for freedom and who understood that the right to vote, to participate in the electoral process was of supreme importance. Somewhere, they must be ecstatic."

All this notwithstanding, we must remain vigilant and cautiously optimistic. When the Reverend Sharpton was asked, since we now have a black president, do we still need you to continue your work of civil rights advocacy? He said certainly! Even though we now have Barack Obama in the White House, there is a greater need for the work of Civil Rights advocates, for we need to keep the new President honest and focused on issues of concern to African Americans, everyone else does it. Thank God for Michele!

Nevertheless, let us not forget, while nearly fifty-two million people voted for Barack Obama, more than forty million voted for John McCain. In these troubling times, many a vote cast was done so against Obama. Let us also realize, from the time of the election, gun sales have risen tremendously and this should be a reason for black people to pray and celebrate, but also keep an eye on the ammunition. Remember, as my Professor used to say, "Every good night ain't gone to sleep." Or, "Every shut eye doesn't mean sleep."

All thing being equal, we need to again remind the President-elect, as he tackles the myriad of problems facing the nation, he must keep in mind the notion of "fair share." That is, despite what is being said about "Affirmative Action," because of historic discrimination there ought to be proportionate appointments in the various department of government to advance the opportunities of minorities, physically challenged, and women. In recent months, Secretary of State Condoleezza Rice criticized the lack of black representation in the Foreign Service, the State Department and in the high echelons of national law enforcement and security. There should be more minority appointments to the various departments, on boards, authorities, and the federal Supreme, Circuit and Appeals Courts. In fact, the nation should be proportionately represented by all its various ethnicities and in this way; America will truly reflect its great diversity. Until then, we must Thank God, all who prayed for and supported Barack Obama, and even those who voted against him, for their efforts forced him to reach within, with God's help, and when the going got tough, he got going. Therefore, we must also Thank Senator Barack Obama, now President–Elect of the United States of America.

Barack Obama: A Concluding Perspective

By Dr. Fred Monderson

Now elected, former Senator Barack Obama from Illinois faces his biggest challenges from the proverbial left, right and center, and from abroad. After all, he has to restore American credibility abroad and try to gain consensus to help solve global problems of economics, security, terrorism, nuclear proliferation, trade concerns and poverty. Now, while the President-Elect has been quick to point out "there's only one President at a time," he has employed that brilliant mind of his in choosing an excellent team after deliberate consideration. Even opponents are praising his choices for the important departments that will help him govern in a meaningful manner, as the American people are hoping he would. However, while some in government have applauded his choice for the important Secretaries for State, Commerce, Defense, and National Security, the United Nations, and Attorney General, some "fifth wheels to the coach," have continued to stonewall in a manner, not constructive or conducive to progress, inasmuch as Barack is trying to fix problems created by his predecessors.

Senator Joe Biden of Delaware, now Vice-President-Elect, rightly predicted, Senator Obama, now President-Elect Obama, would be "tested" within months of his new administration. However, the current challenges, while on President Bush's watch and threatens to spill over into President Obama's, are also important for perception of the kind of president Obama will make, for a number of reasons. First of all, as these are new, and while many have given up on economic changes by the Bush Administration, they expect President-Elect Obama to have meaningful impact on the economy even though constitutionally he can't. Notwithstanding, while staying abreast of developments through White House briefings, Obama's team is also acting as a "shadow cabinet" by studying the issues and creating "real-life models" that can be implemented on day one, when he takes office. Equally important, the "breathing space" gained in the transition, allows the incoming administration to fine tune and "perfect" its approach to get the nation's economy moving, by planning job increases through infrastructure repairs to bridges, roads, tunnels, housing starts; restoration of bank credits for homes, automobiles and other large item purchases. The nation's railways also need overhauling. In a way then, the delay is good in that evolving approaches are focusing on the problems. Still some argue, "We can't wait!" until January 20th, but we must!

The actions of terrorists as in the recent attacks in Mumbai, India, not only convey to the world, the vicious and indiscriminate nature of terrorism and why everyone should be united against this anarchy. This also allows Obama's foreign policy team to prepare to be "ahead of the terrorist curve."

The various coalition groups who made the Obama victory are content to wait and see, thrusting to Mr. Obama's judgment to appoint the best people; craft the best policies for change; fulfill some of his campaign promises such as universal health care; make sure "no child is truly left behind;" put the nation back to work; forestall foreclosures; expand housing starts; shoring up banks to issue credit; closing the controversial Guantanamo Bay Prison which has been a blight on the American domestic and international reputation, that will signal to the world a new administration is human rights conscious; build more schools with state of the art technology, teaching skills, and provide more pay for teachers; cross the aisle to work with progressive Republicans to push legislation forward that transforms the American economic and social landscape to bring about the needed changes.

President Barack Obama's foreign policy and counter-terrorism teams will assist his efforts to repair America's image abroad, and, in consort with our allies, give more badly needed attention to terrorists, states that sponsor terrorism and others bent on harming America and Americans. He must also keep his promise to "Bring the boys and girls home" from Iraq, or at least demonstrate significant drawdown within an acceptable timeframe. He must also shore up the Afghanistan front, and keep a watchful eye on emerging events in the India-Pakistan arena as well as insisting Pakistan move more forcefully against terrorists who cross the Afghanistan border from that nation. As leader of the "Free World" he must devise a strategy to deal with the Pirates of Somalia who threaten the sea lanes in that part of the world. As such, then, beyond the honeymoon period, and within a year, certainly by two years, there ought to be significant turnaround. Thereafter, all things being equal, the President can turn his attention to appointing two or three Supreme Court judges who will protect the ramifications of *Roe v. Wade*, rule in favor of stem-cell research, protect affirmative action, continue to speak out against racist behaviors, and most important, make permanent the Voting Rights Act, that has to be renewed every 25 years. All this, notwithstanding, the presumption is that President Obama would want to encourage the long-held American tradition of civil, social and judicial activism that has characterized societal progress in the realms of justice and equality for blacks and white; low, middle and upper classes; the various ethnicities; young and old; Christians, Jews, Muslims agnostics, etc.; Native Americans; gays, lesbians, handicaps; labor unions, and all aspects of the American social and body politic, as these must remain front burner issues in this new society being crafted.

President Obama must go even further, he must deal with the problems of global warming, environmental protection, insist on better quality automobile emissions and fuel performance, craft a   far-reaching energy policy, encourage the teaching of science and mathematics in the school, and pursue vigorously research and development in science and other areas. We urge he be more considerate towards Native Americans, prison reform, and work to ensure prisoners who have served their time and paid their debt to society are allowed to retain the right to vote, a fundamental tenet of American citizenship. Even more important, however, the plight of black families must be addressed from protection of Civil Rights gains from that torturous campaign, to poverty, destruction of the black family due to racism, discrimination, joblessness, and even excessive incarceration of this ethnic group. Libraries, homelessness, the plight of inner cities must be addressed, as well as Veteran's medical, educational and financial care, and a workable immigration policy that must be considerate enough to bring illegals out of hiding into the comfort of American civil and constitutional protections. When a significant proportion of these items are addressed, the new political phenomenon will certainly be re-elected and promoted to that class of the greatest American presidents. ("Barack Obama: A Concluding Perspective" New York *Daily Challenge* Newspaper, December 11, 2008, pp. 4-5).

www.ingramcontent.com/pod-product-compliance
Lightning Source LLC
Chambersburg PA
CBHW031258280526
45784CB00004B/1891